Taking the NREMT test or State EMT exam can be a painless experience if you are prepared with the knowledge of the course material AND an understanding of what to expect of the NREMT test itself. We have created this page to aid in answering some of the more common questions associated with taking NREMT and state EMT certification tests. This includes facts and advice related to taking and passing the exams. It is intended to aid the EMT candidate in his or her pursuit of certification and registration as an EMT, AEMT, or Paramedic.

Many states have adopted the NREMT cognitive exam as their state exam, however there are a few states that still hold their own exam. The information given here is more specific for the NREMT Computer Adaptive Test (CAT), however the test taking tips are useful for any exam. If you are not going to be taking the NREMT exam, you should contact the state EMS office where you will be testing and see if they provide a study guide for their exam. These study guides are very useful for state specific exams.

Over the years the NREMT exam format has changed from a linear exam (paper and pencil) to the CAT exam. This is an adaptive exam and will vary in length. It is not graded like a traditional linear exam.

Facts That You Need To Know About The NREMT Exam

- NREMT test questions are multiple choice with 4 potential answers. A committee of 10-20 EMS experts, who must all agree that the question is in line with the most current practice analysis study, creates all questions. These EMS experts make sure that there is only one "best" or "correct" answer, and that "each incorrect answer has some level of plausibility." Additionally, each question and answer must be easily found in common text books used in teaching EMS classes.

- As of January 1, 2007 the NREMT has changed its exam formatting to a CBT (Computer Based Testing) method. Exams will no longer be delivered via a paper test and completed with a pencil. All testing will be performed at a computer workstation. PearsonVue testing centers all over the United States administer these tests.

- The CBT that the NREMT is now utilizing is called CAT or (Computer Adaptive Testing) and each exam is tailored specifically to the individual EMT candidate. This testing method is considered state of the art and uses a theory called IRT (Item Response Theory). IRT is a statistical way to measure a person's ability based on the fact that the probability of a person answering a question correctly is directly related to their ability and the difficulty level of the question. Combining CAT with IRT should make NREMT exams more precise, fair, and accurate. What does that mean? Basically each item (question) is given a weighted point value. This value is based on the difficulty of the question. A harder question has a higher point value. An easier question has a lower value.

- New CAT NREMT tests will deliver questions one at a time to the candidate and will NOT be randomly chosen. They are rated along the same ability scale as the candidate is exhibiting proficiency. The first questions on the exam are generally just below the passing standard. If a question is asked that is below the candidate's level of ability, the probability is high for the candidate to answer the question correctly. If a question asked is above a candidate's level of ability, they have a high probability of missing it. If the candidate answers the question correctly then a slightly more difficult question will be delivered next. As the difficulty of the questions increase, eventually the candidate will start to miss questions. The questions then become slightly easier and the candidate will begin to answer correctly again. At this point in the exam the application algorithm calculates an ability estimate for this candidate and begins delivering questions that are slightly harder and slightly easier than the candidate's ability. As the CAT exam progresses, the ability estimate gets more and more precise as the pattern of right to wrong answers stabilizes around the client's true ability. The exam will end at the point when there is a 95% certainty that the candidate's true ability is above or below the passing standard. It can also end if you run out of questions or time, however both of these instances are rare.

- CAT and IRT match the question difficulty to the candidate's perceived level of ability, this limits the number of questions delivered as well as increases accuracy.

- Exam fees can be paid online at the NREMT website, but you must first be registered and sign into your account. You can pay by credit card, or with a payment voucher if your school provides one. You may also mail in payment, however this will delay your ability to schedule your exam until the payment has cleared.

- If you do not pass the exam you may retake it after 14 days. This period is to provide you with time to study.

- NREMT test results are generally available within 1 to 2 business days on the NREMT website. Check your exam results here www.nremt.org

Advice On How To Take And Pass The NREMT Exam And State EMT Tests

This advice has been gleaned from dozens of sources. Information contained here has been compiled from interviews with EMTs and Paramedics who have taken and passed the tests multiple times. It has also been gathered from EMS related discussion forums and nationally recognized test-taking authorities.

What Material To Study For The NREMT Exam

- Technically, you should know everything that was covered in the EMT course materials. There aren't any secret methods or insights that can replace proper test preparation, but some things are common. The tests are heavy in the basics. Know CPR and shock as well as all of the segment categories of the test itself i.e. Airway, Ventilation and Oxygenation; Trauma; Cardiology; Medical; and Operations. Know the major components of the airway and the normal ranges of respiration for adults and pediatric patients. Know diabetic emergencies and the various causes of syncope. You will see about 15% of your questions related to pediatrics, and about 85% related to adults. These will be spread out through the 5 categories listed above.

- A large portion of the exam is related to operations and many students overlook this. Since September 11, 2001 a great effort has been made to incorporate more education about NIMS and ICS with regard to EMS. Understand how these systems work and how they apply to a mass casualty and you will be a step ahead of other candidates.

- The NREMT exam is NOT based upon the textbook you used in your class. The exam is based upon the NREMT Practice Analysis done every five years. The exam questions are written to fall within the Department of Transportation EMT Curriculum. EMT textbooks only give you their interpretation of those standards. (NOTE: The new National EMS Education Standards are EMR (Emergency Medical Responder), EMT, AEMT (Advanced EMT), and Paramedic.)

- Remember, although the NREMT exam looks for a minimum entry-level competency, nobody wants a "just made it by the skin of their teeth" partner. Know your stuff. The more knowledge you have about EMS, the shorter your test will be. If you are answering questions well above the competency line, your exam will end closer to the minimum number of questions rather than the maximum number of questions.

- Obviously take advantage of the EMT and Paramedic Practice Tests here in this book and on the website. There is detailed score tracking and exam review features that let you see your strong and weak areas while you continue to take exams and improve. Identify your strong and weak areas so you can study to improve all around. Use online information resources like Wikipedia to help broaden your subject knowledge and branch out from the knowledge of a single textbook.

Before Taking The NREMT Exam Or State Test

- Eat a well balanced diet and drink plenty of water the day before. Include B vitamin foods like bananas, oatmeal, and raisins, and get plenty of rest. Reschedule if you are sick. Don't attempt the test if you aren't feeling your best.

- Don't cram! If you don't know it the night before the test, you will most likely not know it for the test. Relax or sleep instead of cramming.

- Don't consume a bunch of coffee or sugar before the exam it will only make your anxiety worse. Studies show that consuming caffeine and/or sugar actually slows your brain down and results in lower grades on exams.

- Study regularly for a few weeks before you test. Use the resources from this website, and any other resources you might have to study. Identify your weak areas and then focus your learning in those areas. If possible, you should study for a couple of weeks after completing your EMS course, and then test. Don't wait a long time if you have the ability to test sooner.

- Know exactly where the test center is and arrive early to eliminate the stress of being late. Remember, you have to be signed up for the test. You cannot just walk in and take it. Bring your photo ID and a couple of pencils. Scrap paper will be provided for you and it must be turned in with your exam.

- When you go to take the test dress in multiple layers so that you can shed what you do not need and still be comfortable. Temperatures of testing centers can vary a great deal throughout the day especially if it is a rarely used room or building. Being nervous will cause your vessels to constrict and you will feel colder than you might normally feel. Shivering during a test is no fun!

- Go to the bathroom before the test. You are allowed to go during the exam, but take care of it sooner rather than later. If you have to leave the testing room you will be required to take one form of ID with you while the other stays within the testing center, and it will be verified each time you leave and enter.

- You must bring two forms of ID to the exam site, and at least one of them must have a photo ID.

During The NREMT Exam Or State Test

- You CANNOT skip a question and come back to it later. The nature of the CAT exam requires that you answer each question individually before any additional questions are delivered. The next question you get delivered is based on how you answered the previous questions. This is why you must make a choice before you can proceed.

- Look out for words like EXCEPT, ALWAYS, NEVER, MOST APPROPRIATE and other qualifiers. Anything that puts limits on the potential answer should be a flag to slow down and read the question and all answers very carefully.

- Read the whole question thoroughly at least a couple of times and formulate the answer in your head BEFORE you look at the answer choices. If you look at the answer choices prior to understanding the question completely, you can be lead to choose an incorrect answer. The test is timed, but by slowing down, you will actually have a shorter test. Don't worry about the time, worry about making the correct choice.

- For each question there are 4 potential answers. All of the choices must have some plausibility to them. It is possible that all 4 choices are correct, or that all 4 choices are wrong. You must choose the "most" correct choice available, even if it is not what you would normally do first.

- Do not complicate the scenario or situation. Do not bring elements into the questions that are not there. This will cause you to overlook the basics, which is probably what the question is testing for.

- Relax, and remember to breath adequately. Slow deep your breath by breathing in through your nose, and then exhaling out through your mouth. Repeat. Do this as often as you find yourself hurrying, rushing, or getting angry.

The NREMT's Newest Test Plan

The National Registry test plan changed on September 1, 2010. The new test plan now covers five topic areas: Airway, Ventilation and Oxygenation; Trauma; Cardiology; Medical and Operations. This plan applies to all national EMS certification levels.

A total of 85% of the exam items cover adult patients and 15% cover pediatric patients. Former items that covered OB are now part of the medical section of the exam. Examinations are not scored on the basis of topic areas (sections). Passing an examination still requires successful demonstration of entry-level competency over the entire domain of the test.

The changes in the test plan are the result of an NREMT research project that prioritized tasks all EMS providers accomplish while providing care. The NREMT test plan is designed to cover the important tasks of the job. The NREMT Board adopted this plan in November of 2009. Items in the test bank are the same items that were in previous test banks. The emphasis is just different because the NREMT adjusted the emphasis of the test based upon EMS provider data.

The NREMT EMR Exam

Has between 80 and 110 questions. You have 1 hour and 45 minutes to complete the exam. Cost of the NREMT EMR Exam is $65.00. The exam will cover the entire spectrum of EMS care including: Airway, Ventilation, Oxygenation; Trauma; Cardiology; Medical; and EMS Operations. Items related to patient care are focused on adult patients (85%) and pediatric patients (15%). In order to pass the exam, you must meet a standard level of competency. The passing standard is defined by the ability to provide safe and effective entry-level emergency medical care.

The NREMT EMT Exam

Has between 70 and 120 questions. You have two hours to complete the test. Cost of the NREMT Exam is $70.00. The exam will cover the entire spectrum of EMS care including: Airway, Ventilation, Oxygenation; Trauma; Cardiology; Medical; and EMS Operations. Items related to patient care are focused on adult patients (85%) and pediatric patients (15%). In order to pass the exam, you must meet a standard level of competency. The passing standard is defined by the ability to provide safe and effective entry-level emergency medical care.

The NREMT AEMT Exam

Is a Computer Based Test (CBT). There are 135 questions that each candidate must answer in 2 hours and 15 minutes. The exam will cover the entire spectrum of EMS care including: Airway, Respiration & Ventilation; Cardiology & Resuscitation; Trauma; Medical & Obstetrics/Gynecology; and EMS Operations. Items related to patient care are focused on adult and geriatric patients (85%) and pediatric patients (15%). In order to pass the exam, you must meet a standard level of competency. The passing standard is defined by the ability to provide safe and effective entry -level advanced emergency medical care.

The NREMT EMT Paramedic Exam

Has between 80 and 150 questions and you have 2 hours and 30 minutes to complete the exam. Cost of the NREMT Paramedic Exam is $110.00. The exam will cover the entire spectrum of EMS care including: Airway, Ventilation, Oxygenation; Trauma; Cardiology; Medical; and EMS Operations. Items related to patient care are focused on adult patients (85%) and pediatric patients (15%). In order to pass the exam, you must meet a standard level of competency. The passing standard is defined by the ability to provide safe and effective entry-level emergency medical care.

How NREMT Exams and Questions are Constructed

Most of the National Exams given in the United States follow the formula below in developing questions. The NREMT is one of these tests. If you start to understand what type of questions you are being asked, it will allow you to begin to know how to apply the correct response. This is some deep reading, but has helped many people in their test taking. Read through the information, and then see if you can start to figure it out as you take practice tests. We will try to give a few examples at the end.

In 1956, Benjamin Bloom headed a group of educational psychologists who developed a classification of levels of intellectual behavior important in learning. Bloom found that over 95% of the test questions students encountered required them to think only at the lowest possible level...the recall of information.

Bloom identified six levels within the cognitive domain, from the simple recall or recognition of facts as the lowest level, through increasingly more complex and abstract mental levels, to the highest order, which is classified as evaluation. Verb examples that represent intellectual activity on each level are listed here.

1. Knowledge: arrange, define, duplicate, label, list, memorize, name, order, recognize, relate, recall, repeat, reproduce, state.

2. Comprehension: classify, describe, discuss, explain, express, identify, indicate, locate, recognize, report, restate, review, select, translate.

3. Application: apply, choose, demonstrate, dramatize, employ, illustrate, interpret, operate, practice, schedule, sketch, solve, use, write.

4. Analysis: analyze, appraise, calculate, categorize, compare, contrast, criticize, differentiate, discriminate, distinguish, examine, experiment, question, test.

5. Synthesis: arrange, assemble, collect, compose, construct, create, design, develop, formulate, manage, organize, plan, prepare, propose, set up, write.

6. Evaluation: appraise, argue, assess, attach, choose, compare, defend, estimate, judge, predict, rate, core, select, support, value, evaluate.

The chart below shows the increasing level of complexity of question construction.

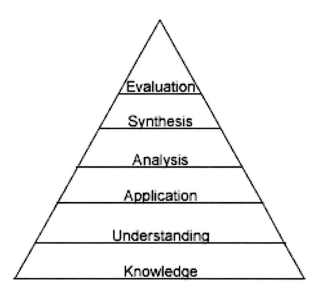

The NREMT exam follows a similar formula in that it starts with the basic Knowledge then begins to increase the style of question to determine the candidate's true grasp of a subject. This is why you will see similar questions during the test. Questions will be written in a slightly different way to see if you truly grasp the concept around it.

Questions given during your training are questions in the "knowledge" category 80% to 90% of the time. These questions are not bad, but using them all the time is. Instructors should try to utilize higher order level of questions. These questions require much more "brain power" and a more extensive and elaborate answer. Below are the six question categories as defined by Bloom. After each one is an example of how the question would be worded (started) so that you can begin to decipher at what level this question is being formed.

KNOWLEDGE
- Remembering;
- Memorizing;
- Recognizing;
- Recalling identification
- Recall of information
  - Who, what, when, where, how ...?
  - Describe

COMPREHENSION
- Interpreting;
- Translating from one medium to another;
- Describing in one's own words;
- Organization and selection of facts and ideas
  - Retell...

APPLICATION
- Problem solving;
- Applying information to produce some result;
- Use of facts, rules, and principles;
  - How is...an example of ...?
  - How is...related to ...?
  - Why is...significant?

ANALYSIS

- Subdividing something to show how it is put together;
- Finding the underlying structure of a communication;
- Identifying motives;
- Separation of a whole into component parts;
  - What are the parts or features of ...?
  - Classify...according to...
  - Outline/Diagram...
  - How does...compare/contrast with...?
  - What evidence can you list ...?

SYNTHESIS
- Creating a unique, original product that may be in verbal form or may be a physical object;
- Combination of ideas to form a new whole;
  - What would you predict/infer from...?
  - What ideas can you add to...?
  - How would you create/design a new...?
  - What might happen if you combined...?
  - What solutions would you suggest for...?

EVALUATION
- Making value decisions about issues;
- Resolving controversies or differences of opinion;
- Development of opinions, judgments, or decisions
  - Do you agree...?
  - What do you think about...?
  - What is the most important...?
  - Place the following in order of priority...
  - How would you decide about...?
  - What criteria would you use to assess...?

This is the nuts and bolts of how an NREMT exam is built. Below is an example of how an NREMT question is constructed. This will give you some insight into the thinking behind each question.

Steps to Question Writing

A well-designed multiple-choice item consists of three main components: a stem (asks a question or poses a statement which requires completion), key (the correct answer/s), and distracter(s) (incorrect option/s). The following section is designed to enhance the candidate's understanding of the NREMT question writing process.

Step 1. Select an area of the test plan for the focus of the item.
* Patient Assessment

Step 2. Select a subcategory from the chosen area of the test plan.
* Multiple patient incidents

Step 3. Select an important concept within that subcategory.
* Assess and triage among a group of patients to prioritize the order of care delivery

Step 4. Use the concept selected and write the stem.
* The EMT arrives on scene of a vehicle accident.
Which is the most critical patient that should be transported first?

Step 5. Write a key to represent important information the entry-level EMT should know.
* Altered Level of Consciousness
~ A patient who doesn't remember the accident or what the day is

Step 6. Identify common errors, misconceptions, or irrelevant information.
* Distracting injuries
* Smell of alcohol
* Lack of understanding of expected findings related to a specific clinical finding

Step 7. Use the previous information and write the distracters
~ A patient who has a large bleeding gash to the right arm
~ A patient who smells of alcohol and is having trouble walking
~ A patient with moderate Alzheimer's disease (AD) who is asking to talk with the spouse who died several years ago

Step 8. Complete the item using the stem, key, and distracters.
The EMT arrives on scene of a multiple vehicle accident. After assuring scene safety and assessing the patients, whom should the EMT transport first?
1. The patient who doesn't remember the accident or what day it is. (Key)
2. The patient with a large bleeding gash to the right arm.
3. The patient who smells like alcohol and is having trouble walking straight.
4. The patient, whose family states, has moderate Alzheimer's disease and is asking to talk to a spouse who died several years ago.

In this example you can see that the question is asked at the Evaluation level of Bloom's Taxonomy. That is the highest form of question. It requires you to know information about each answer option, and then weigh each against the other to determine an order of care. In this sample question you can see that a patient with an altered level of consciousness would be the most critical given the information you have. A large bleeding gash is a distracting injury, easily treated with bandaging, and not requiring the most immediate transport. A patient who smells like alcohol and is possibly intoxicated does not in itself warrant immediate transport. This would probably be the second most critical due to mechanism and not being able to determine LOC as easily as others. The patient who is asking to speak to a dead spouse has a disease that would make this type of response normal. This is the type of question that the NREMT likes to give. It requires you to really think about each option and only use the information presented in the question and answers.

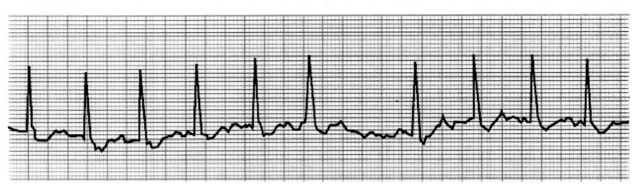

Question 1: You arrive on scene to a patient with chest pain and shortness of breath. Her son tells you she started having chest pain four hours ago and has not been acting normal for the past hour. He also tells you she has had a history of CHF and some heart problems. You attach a monitor and observe this rhythm. She is also breathing approximately 26 bpm, and has a blood pressure of 81/50. Based on this description, what would be the most appropriate treatment for this patient?

a. Cardioversion beginning at 120
b. Diltiazem .25mg/kg
c. Adenosine 6mg
d. Drug administration and cardioversion are both contraindicated in this patient.

Question 2: You are on scene of a motor vehicle accident where the car has left the road and collided with a group of trees. The driver was alone and is out of the car standing on the road. You see that the airbag on the driver's side has deployed. Which of the following recommendations would be best to follow?

a. Do a rapid standing take down of the patient as the mechanism suggests the possibility of a spinal injury.
b. Detach the battery cables to protect you and other rescuers from injury by the passenger side airbag.
c. Lift the airbag away from the steering wheel and look for damage to the steering column and wheel.
d. Have the patient lay down while a proper assessment is performed to determine if spinal immobilization is necessary.

Question 3: Giving a patient nitroglycerin during a cardiac emergency will?

a. Speed up the heart rate
b. Constrict the vessels
c. Dilate the vessels
d. Increase workload on the heart

Question 4: If someone has audible inspiratory stridor they may have _____.

a. CHF
b. An upper airway obstruction
c. Therapeutic oxygen around
d. A lower airway obstruction

Question 5: You and your partner Amber arrive on scene to find a pregnant woman in her 38th week. She feels like she is in active labor and requests transport to the hospital. While your partner takes vital signs in route you are assessing how far along the delivery is. You see the patient has some hemorrhaging from the vagina which leads you to believe she may have_____ or _____ and that she should be transported on her _____.

a. Placenta previa or placenta abruptio / right side
b. A premature delivery or prolapsed umbilical cord /left side
c. Twins or triplets / left side

d. Placenta previa or placenta abruptio / left side

Question 6: You respond to a call of a man down in a very rough neighborhood. Upon entering the location of the call you notice a group of young men in a fist fight at what appears to be the address of the call. There are two men on the ground not moving and your lights and sirens have frightened the other men away. What should you do next?

a. Call for police to secure the scene and wait for them to arrive
b. Treat the patient with the worst injuries first
c. Check to see if they have a weapon
d. Chase down the slowest guy and hold him for the police

Question 7: After doing CPR on a 72 yr old female patient in VF for over 6 minutes she suddenly has a Return of Spontaneous Circulation. After optimizing ventilation you notice her blood pressure is 79/50. Your protocols state to start a Norepinephrine Infusion if the patients blood pressure is below 90 systolic. You guess the patients weight in pounds is 90. According to 2010 ACLS guidelines what would be the correct dose range for a Norepinephrine Infusion for this patient?

a. 1 mg IV Bolus followed by a 20cc flush
b. 9-45 mcg/kg per minute
c. 10-20 mg/kg over 5 minutes
d. 4.05-20.25 mcg/kg per minute

Question 8: The Incident Command System (ICS) is used to:

a. Ensure efficient use of resources, public and responder safety, as well as the successful completion of incident management goals.
b. Ensure that responses to MCI's are rapid, organized, and well managed.
c. Prevent individual agencies from making poor response decisions because of poor communications or lack of resources.
d. Create organizational goals for NIMS during natural disasters, terrorist acts, or Hazmat incidents.

Question 9: You and your partner Wilson arrive on scene to a fire that is under control. You are treating a patient with full thickness burns to the arm. During transport to the helicopter Wilson says, "Hey, what zone of the burn is the part that will recover?" You respond, "The _____.

a. Zone of coagulation
b. Zone of hemoptysis
c. Zone of stasis
d. Zone of hyperemia

Question 10: Medications can be administered through a number of different routes. Which answer choice is NOT one of them?

a. Interstitial
b. Sublingual
c. Intramuscular
d. Inhalation

Question 11: You arrive on scene to find a 62 year old female in cardiac arrest. The fire department has already initiated CPR and attached an AED. You quickly assess the patient for reversible causes. According to the 2010 ACLS guidelines which of the following T's below is not a reversible cause?

a. Toxins
b. Thrombosis-cerebral
c. Thrombosis-coronary
d. Tension Pneumothorax

Question 12: You arrive on scene with your partner Jermain to assist on a mass casualty. You have just begun tending an arterial bleed on a woman who was thrown from a car when you hear the cries of a baby. You have the woman maintain pressure on the bleed with a trauma dressing and go to the car with the infant crying. What did you just do?

a. Abandon a patient
b. Triaged the scene
c. Acted in the best interest of both patients
d. Acted under the guidelines of the Good Samaritan Law

Question 13: You respond to a patient who is short of breath. Upon arrival, you encounter a 54 year old patient who is conscious, alert to your presence and appears oriented. The patient is Diaphoretic and in apparent respiratory distress. She is seated in the tripod position with pursed lips. Your initial treatment consists of high flow oxygen and a baseline set of vitals. Your next course of treatment should include the following?

a. CPAP only
b. RSI
c. 12 lead EKG
d. CPAP with duo-neb treatment

Question 14: You and your partner Janell are just approaching the scene of a two vehicle collision. One of the vehicles is on it's side and the distinct smell of propane can be detected. A high pitch whistling sound can be heard from the overturned vehicle and you can see the driver has been partially ejected through the window. Janell calls for Hazmat as you:

a. Rapidly pull the driver to safety, away from the vehicle
b. Ensure that the ambulance is parked a safe distance from the scene
c. Set up flares to mark the hot zone of the scene to discourage bystanders from entering
d. Begin triage on the most critically injured patient

Question 15: You assess a patient who you believe is not acting rationally. They have an altered LOC and a large gash on the side of their head that is actively bleeding. The patient is adamantly refusing treatment. Which would be the best course of action?

a. Have them sign a patient refusal and leave them at the scene
b. Contact medical control and request police assistance in managing the patient
c. Have your partner sneak up behind them and gently bring them to the ground
d. Explain to them again your request to treat them. If they deny treatment, you must leave.

Question 16: If a patient has a positive QRS in Lead I and a negative QRS in Lead AVF, how would you describe their Axis Deviation?

a. Normal Axis Deviation
b. Left Axis Deviation
c. Extreme Right Axis Deviation
d. Right Axis Deviation

Question 17: You are setting up the landing zone for a helicopter transport of a critical MVA patient. Which of the following would be considered acceptable methods of marking the boundaries of this zone?

a. Reflective tape held down by large rocks
b. Garbage cans with flashlights on top
c. 4 vehicles with their lights pointed inward
d. Sheets tied in between 4 trees

Question 18: According to the 2010 AHA guidelines, how many shocks should be delivered prior to resuming CPR?

a. 1 shock
b. 2 shocks
c. 3 shocks
d. 5 shocks

Question 19: After performing CPR on a 62 year old patient in cardiac arrest, your patient has a return of spontaneous circulation. At what rate are you going to tell your partner to ventilate the patient?

a. Start ventilating the patient at a rate of 10-12 breaths a minute and titrate to achieve a PETCO2 of 35-40mm Hg.
b. Start ventilating the patient at a rate of 8-10 breaths per minute and titrate to achieve a PETCO2 of 30-40mm Hg.
c. Start ventilating the patient at a rate of 6-8 breaths per minute and titrate to achieve a PETCO2 of 35-45mm Hg.
d. Start ventilating the patient at a rate of 12-15 breaths per minute and titrate to achieve a PETCO2 of 30-35mm Hg.

Question 20: What is a contraindication for the use of CPAP?

a. A patient with nausea/vomiting
b. A patient of a near drowning
c. A patient with COPD
d. A patient with CHF

Question 21: A 6 year old girl was found outside in her yard unconscious. She is breathing 6 breaths a minute and her pulse is 58 bpm with poor systematic perfusion. What should you do?

a. Assist ventilations with high flow O2 and transport rapidly
b. Initiate chest compressions and assist ventilations with high flow O2
c. Use an epinephrine auto injector to increase her heart rate
d. Transport with high flow O2 and assist respirations if needed

Question 22: You come upon a victim of asphyxial cardiac arrest. Which of the following is the correct order of action?

a. Activate the emergency response system and then begin CPR
b. Do CPR at a 15:2 rate for 5 minutes and then activate the emergency response system
c. Do CPR for 5 cycles or approximately 2 minutes and then activate the emergency response system and retrieve the AED
d. Retrieve the AED and analyze, then begin CPR

Question 23: Your patient is an unresponsive 44 year old female who has a pulse but is not breathing. How should you proceed with CPR?

a. Immediate chest compressions followed by two rescue breaths
b. 2 quick rescue breaths and then provide 10-12 breaths per minute
c. 2 quick rescue breaths and 12-20 breaths per minute
d. Attach the AED and analyze, then begin CPR

Question 24: What would be an expected systolic BP in infants, toddlers, and preschool aged children?

a. 50 mm Hg
b. 60 mm Hg
c. 70 mm Hg
d. 80 mm Hg

Question 25: Baroreceptors are sensory nerve endings that _____.

a. Manage leukocyte secretions
b. Sense changes in blood pressure
c. Sense drops in interstatial fluid levels
d. Manage the opening and closing of alveoli

Question 26: What are two contraindications for the use of a Combitube?

a. Burned face/Gag reflex
b. Under 18/Unconscious
c. You don't have lubricant/The patient has the flu
d. The patient is under 4ft tall/You know they have esophageal disease

Question 27: A freight car has overturned and is spilling hundreds of gallons of hazardous chemicals into a local creek. Incident Command has told you that the toxicity of the hazardous material is a level 3. What level of protection must any personnel entering this area be wearing?

a. Level 1 protection
b. Level C protection
c. Level D protection
d. Level A or B protection

Question 28: You and your partner Bill arrive on scene to a head on collision involving 2 cars. After making sure the scene was safe, your partner moves to the first car to open the patient's airway. What technique should Bill use to do this?

a. Laryngoscope
b. Trendelenburg tilt
c. Head tilt chin lift
d. Jaw thrust

Question 29: In a 3rd degree heart block the P R interval will be?

a. Shorter than .20 seconds
b. Longer than .20 seconds
c. Little spikes
d. Variant

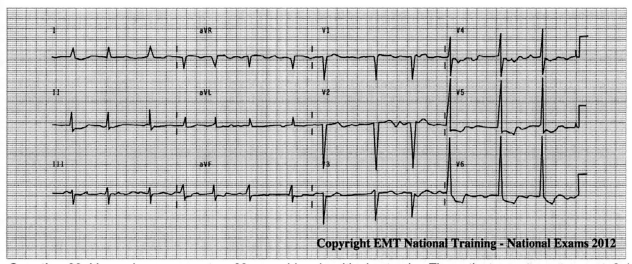

Question 30: You arrive on scene to a 63 year old male with chest pain. The patient reports acute onset, 8-10, and crushing substernal chest pain which he rates 8 out of 10. The patient is pale, cool, diaphoretic, and short of breath. He reports onset of symptoms 20 minutes ago while watching TV. He denies any cardiac history. The patient is breathing 22 times a minute and has an oxygen saturation of 92%. Your partner reports a blood pressure of 110/55. You have your partner apply oxygen, while you obtain a 12-lead. Which of the following answers below is the correct ECG interpretation?

a. Inferior Infarction
b. Anterior Ischemia
c. Septal Infarction
d. Lateral Ischemia

Question 31: The incident commander has put you in control of a night time medivac of a cardiac arrest patient. Which of the following would be considered appropriate?

a. Secure all equipment and supplies that could become airborne
b. Set up the landing lights in a square approximately 50 feet X 50 feet
c. As the helicopter approaches the landing zone, shine lights on hazardous obstacles like power lines and leaning trees
d. Mark a giant X on the ground with rocks

Question 32: An ambulance unit or fire department that makes an uncoordinated, independent decision during an incident is said to be:

a. Soloing
b. Spear Heading
c. Bird Dogging
d. Freelancing

Question 33: Which of the following is true of BiPAP?

a. BiPAP provides one type of pressure
b. BiPAP is similar to CPAP when the patient exhales
c. BiPAP is a leak tolerant system
d. BiPAP combines partial ventilatory support and PEEP

Question 34: Which of the following combines partial ventilatory support and CPAP?

a. Endotracheal intubation
b. PEEP
c. Venturri Mask
d. Biphasic positive airway pressure

Question 35: You are called to a neighborhood pool where a 5 year old girl was found floating unconscious. She is cyanotic and has no muscle tone. Your partner Greg does not find a pulse and the child is not breathing. Your CPR should include a compression to ventilation ratio of_____ and each compression should be at a depth of_____.

a. 15:2 / one third to one half the depth of the chest
b. 15:2 / one third of the anterior-posterior diameter of the chest
c. 30:2 / 1.5 to 2 inches in depth
d. 15:2 / just enough to give adequate chest rise

Question 36: You arrive on scene of a 62 year old male with acute onset of chest pain. The patient states he was walking down his driveway to get the mail when his chest begin to hurt. The origin of the pain is substernal and it is radiating to his jaw and down his left arm. You tell your partner to take vitals and you attach the monitor. You print the four lead and immediately notice 3mm ST elevation in lead II. From this information what do you immediately know?

a. Patient is having a myocardial infarction
b. Patient has a right bundle branch block
c. Patient is having a ischemic episode
d. You do not have enough information to make an informed decision

Question 37: Incident Command has put you in charge of setting up the landing zone for a helicopter transport. What size area will you try to procure for this zone? What is the minimum acceptable size for this zone?

a. 500 ft X 500 ft / minimum of 250 feet X 250 feet
b. 100 feet X 100 feet / minimum of 60 feet X 60 feet
c. 50 feet X 50 feet / minimum of 25 feet X 25 feet
d. 25 feet X 25 feet / minimum of 15 feet by 15 feet

Question 38: You are dispatched to a cardiac arrest. Your patient is a 56 year old female who collapsed at a funeral. Upon arrival your EMT partner begins CPR while you hook up the monitor and start an IV in the left AC. After 2 minutes of CPR you stop and check the patient's rhythm and note that she is in v-fib. You deliver 1 shock and your partner immediately continues CPR. After 30 seconds you then administer 1mg of Epinephrine. Your partner finishes 5 cycles of CPR and you check the monitor and see a sinus rhythm. What is the next step you should take?

a. Analyze the rhythm to determine your next intervention
b. Start ROSC protocol
c. Check the patient's pulse
d. Continue CPR and administer 300mg Amiodarone via IV push

Question 39: All of the following are considered stimulants except:

a. Phentermine hydrochloride
b. Amphetamine
c. Diazepam
d. PCP

Question 40: A train derailment has caused two tanker cars to explode and several others to begin leaking an unknown gas. The size of the affected area is large and crosses several county lines. According to NIMS, this type of MCI would benefit most from a:

a. Multiple Command System
b. Unified Command System
c. Singular Command System
d. Coordinated Command System

Question 41: When administering oxygen to a patient with COPD experiencing diffuse chest pain and shortness of breath, you should?

a. Place a mask on the patient but do not turn on the oxygen
b. You do not administer oxygen any differently than you would to any other patient
c. Reduce oxygen from the usual 85-100% to between 25-35%
d. You must deliver higher percentage of oxygen because the patient has COPD

Question 42: You and your partner Maria have just started CPR on a 23 year old MVA victim. According to AHA CPR guidelines how often should you change compressor roles?

a. Every 1 minute
b. Every 2 minutes
c. Every 5 minutes
d. Every 10 minutes

Question 43: An Incident Command System is designed to:

a. Notify emergency personnel about the level of triage to expect
b. Stabilize patients of a mass casualty
c. Define the roles and responsibilities of an EMS system
d. Manage and control emergency responders and resources

Question 44: You are called to a scene of a 3-year-old who is not breathing and is pulseless. Your CPR should include compressions at what depth?

a. 1-2 inches
b. 1.5-2.5 inches
c. At least 1/3rd the depth of the chest
d. No compressions, it's a child

Question 45: You are the first EMS unit on scene of a multiple casualty incident. A crane has fallen from a building roof top and ripped through an adjacent building. What should you do according to the ICS?

a. Notify dispatch of the need for an Incident Commander and begin triaging patients.
b. Inform IC of your location and begin triaging patients if the scene is safe.
c. Stay a safe distance from the incident and do what the Incident Commander tells you to do.
d. Take incident command until relieved or reassigned

Question 46: The structure of an incident command system:

a. Is broken down by the degree of distress or trauma associated with the event
b. Can contain multiple sectors, but only one incident commander
c. Is decided at the scene by the safety officer
d. Is not effective at organizing agencies from different areas

Question 47: What is the proper sequence of intubating a patient?

a. Check equipment, insert tube, deflate cuff, and remove laryngoscope
b. Check equipment, inflate tube, insert tube, and remove laryngoscope
c. Deflate cuff, insert tube, check equipment, and high flow O2
d. Check equipment, insert tube, remove laryngoscope, and inflate cuff

Question 48: An adult with a respiration rate of _____per minute would be considered within normal limits. A child aged 3-5 with a respiration rate of_____per minute would be considered within normal limits and an infant who is breathing at_____per minute would be considered within normal limits.

a. 22, 32, 42
b. 11, 6, 15
c. 20, 40, 60
d. 16, 25, 40

Question 49: You are called to treat a 69 year old male who has fallen and lost consciousness. He has a laceration on his head and is breathing very rapidly. Which of the following is a likely cause?

a. He has hypoglycemia
b. He has had a heart attack
c. He has slipped and hit his head
d. All of the above

Question 50: You and your partner have been called by law enforcement to a residence for an apparent case of physical child abuse. Upon entering the dwelling you see a 3 or 4-year-old boy sitting with a female officer. During assessment you notice bruising on the child's stomach and chest. The child says he fell off the trampoline. What is your primary concern on this scene?

a. Make sure that the child is removed from the house where the abuse happened.
b. Help law enforcement verify the abuse so that the person who did it is held accountable.
c. Verification that the child was not hit or kicked anywhere in the head.
d. Recognizing the potential for internal injuries based on the bruises located on the child's stomach and chest.

Question 51: What range of degrees is Left Axis Deviation?

a. 0 to -90 degrees
b. 0 to 90 degrees
c. 90 to 180 degrees
d. -90 to -180 degrees

Question 52: After treating a patient in cardiac arrest the patient has a return of spontaneous circulation (ROSC). The patients blood pressure is below 80 systolic and you prepare to begin a Dopamine infusion. What is the correct formula?

a. .2-.10 mcg/kg per minute
b. 5-10 mcg/kg per minute
c. 2-10 mcg/kg per minute
d. .1-.5 mcg/kg per minute

Question 53: Your patient is a 65 year old male with chest pain. As you attach the cardiac monitor he becomes unresponsive and pulseless. Your cardiac monitor shows ventricular fibrillation. According to 2010 ACLS guidelines what is the correct sequence of steps to follow when treating this patient?

a. Defibrillate, CPR 30:2, 1mg Epinepherine, check pulse
b. Began CPR, defibrillate when monitor is ready, continue CPR 30:2, 40 units of vasopressin
c. Began CPR 30:2, 1mg epinepherine, check rhythm, defibrillate
d. Defibrillate, CPR 30:2, 300mg Amiodarone, rapid transport

Question 54: Your patient is a 74 year old female who had an episode of syncope. You attach a cardiac monitor, note sinus bradycardia, and make the decision to administer Atropine. If multiple doses are needed, how long do you need to wait between each dose?

a. 1-3 minutes
b. 3-5 minutes
c. You can only administer Atropine once
d. 5-7 minutes

Question 55: Which of the following answers below would help you identify that a patient has Wolff-Parkinson-White Syndrome?

a. It can only be identified on a 12 lead in V1 and V2. Patient will have widened QRS.
b. If the patient has Paroxysmal SVT.
c. Anterior Hemiblock in leads I, II, and aVf.
d. Consistent rhythm of Delta Waves.

Question 56: You arrive on scene to a patient that has a history of anxiety. She has not been taking her medications as prescribed. As you look at her medication list you notice she is prescribed Diazepam, what drug is this commonly known as?

a. Xanax
b. Ativan
c. Valium
d. Versed

Question 57: You arrive on scene to a find 2 EMT's performing CPR on a 76 year old male in cardiac arrest. You attach the cardiac monitor and began assessing the patient for reversible causes. According to the 2010 ACLS guidelines which of the following H's is not a reversible cause?

a. Hyperthermia
b. Hypoxia
c. Hypokalemia
d. Hydrogen ion

Question 58: You arrive on scene to a 71 year old male with shortness of breath and chest pain. He informs you he has a history of A-fib and is prescribed Warfarin but has not taken it in the last 3 days and has no history of respiratory problems. When you take his vitals you notice he is breathing at a rate of 26 per minute, SPO2 is 89%, he is tachycardic with an irregular rhythm and is hypotensive. You administer oxygen and start an IV. When you reassess his vitals after 5 minutes you notice the patient has not improved and his SPO2 reading has dropped to 87%. Based on this information what might be happening to this patient?

a. Respiratory Distress Syndrome
b. Onset of CHF
c. Acute Myocardial Infarction
d. Pulmonary Embolism

Question 59: Your patient is an 86 year old woman who states she is feeling "funny and light headed." As you are talking with her she becomes unresponsive and apneic. What should you immediately do?

a. Check her blood glucose level
b. Auscultate her lungs
c. Begin ventilations with a Bag-Mask Device
d. Assess her pulse

Question 60: One pupil dilated and the other constricted would suggest what type of injury?

a. Cervical
b. Cerebral
c. Crovasic
d. Cellular

Question 61: Your patient is a 14 year old girl who is complaining of vaginal pain after falling onto the center post of her bike. She is alone and very scared. She has called the accident in on her cell phone and stated that she is bleeding very badly and feeling faint. Besides treating for shock, what other things should you consider with this patient?

a. Transporting in the fowler's position - O2 on nasal canula at 6 lpm
b. Parental release - advice about bike riding
c. If she is having her period - are her parents home
d. Having a female EMT respond for the patient's modesty

Question 62: In which 2 leads on a 12 lead can you commonly identify a Left Bundle Branch Block (LBBB)?

a. Leads V3, V5
b. Leads V5, V6
c. Leads V2, V3
d. Leads V2, V6

Question 63: You arrive on scene to a 74 year old who is having a COPD exacerbation. You have about a 45 minute transport to the hospital. As part of your treatment, medical direction has ordered you to administer Methylprednisolone, what is this drug commonly known as?

a. Albuterol
b. Solu-Medrol
c. Atrovent
d. Terbutaline

Question 64: A postictal state can be accompanied by deep rapid breathing that is meant to burn off excess C02 in the body. This state, prior to the elimination of CO2, could be referred to as?

a. Metabolic alkalosis
b. Respiratory alkalosis
c. Metabolic acidosis
d. Respiratory acidosis

Question 65: Typically atrial fibrillation will present with a tachycardic response when observing an EKG. Which prescribed medication slows the rate of A-fib?

a. Nitroglycerin
b. Propranolol
c. Digoxin
d. Warfin

Question 66: HIPAA stands for _____.

a. Health investigation pontification and accessibility act
b. Hydrointraparieatel angioaduction
c. Hemostasis. infection - pathogen - allergen - antihistamine
d. Health insurance portability and accountability act

Question 67: You arrive on scene with your partner Wayne to find a man at a bowling alley in respiratory distress. He is walking around looking pale and acting agitated. Audible wheezing sounds can be heard as he breathes in. His cousin says he was just getting ready to bowl when he started coughing and now it's like this. You ask the man if he is choking and he wheezes "yes". What should you do for this patient?

a. Use a pair of Magill forceps to remove the blockage
b. Heimlich maneuver
c. Transport and encourage him to cough
d. Wait until he passes out from choking then do compressions to dislodge the food

Question 68: When treating hypotension during return of spontaneous circulation (ROSC) following cardiac arrest, how much and what type of IV bolus does the 2010 ACLS guidelines recommend?

a. 2-4L, Lactated Ringer's
b. 1-3L, Colloid Solution
c. 1-2L, D50
d. 1-2L Normal Saline

Question 69: Indications of CPAP would include all of the following except?

a. Asthma
b. CHF
c. Emphysema
d. Unable to tolerate mask

Question 70: Your patient is a 44 year old male who appears to be having an allergic reaction to shrimp. He is pale and diaphoretic with diffuse erythema and urticaria on his trunk. He has his own Epipen, but has not used it. His pulse is 100 and his BP is 90/50. He states he is taking 40mg of nebivolol a day. He also tells you that he is beginning to have difficulty swallowing. Which of the following would be the best treatment and why?

a. Administer epinephrine and prepare suction. Epinephrine and nebivolol often cause nausea and vomiting.
b. Administer epinephrine and prepare to give an additional dosage. Patients taking nebivolol may require more epinephrine.
c. Administer O2 via NRB enroute to ER. Epinephrine should not be administered to patients taking nebivolol.
d. Administer abdominal thrusts in order to expel the shrimp from his throat. Once removed, transport to nearest hospital.

Question 71: You are called to a boat launch at Lake Santa Cruz for a 36-year-old female who has fallen and injured her leg. You arrive to find a female patient with extreme pain in the left thigh. She is lying on the dock screaming while several people who are drinking beer offer their advice. You direct your team to apply a traction splint because you find:

a. External rotation of the injured extremity
b. Deformity proximal to the knee of the injured extremity
c. Palpable deformity mid-shaft in the injured femur
d. The patient is in need of pain relief

Question 72: You and your partner Gertrude arrive on scene to find two men who have been in a fist fight and have been handcuffed by police. You have been asked to treat both men. While Gertrude is treating one man for facial lacerations and a contusion on the head, the man begins to have a seizure. What would you do?

a. Make sure your patient was in equal or adequate care and call for more backup to assist.
b. Make sure your patient was in equal or more advanced care and then assist Gertrude with airway management
c. Get your patient loaded up and on the way to the hospital and then help Gertrude
d. Prepare to suction Gertrude's patient and get back to the other guy that is less priority

Question 73: You have been unsuccessful in starting an IV on a 2 year old child that is in cardiac arrest. Your medical direction indicates you should consider initiating IO access to administer medications. As you prepare this procedure what are the anatomical landmarks you are looking for, and what are the complication risks with this procedure?

a. distal tibia / fracture of the tibia
b. proximal tibia / pulmonary embolism
c. distal fibula / compartment syndrome
d. proximal fibula / severe pain

Question 74: Which of the following is a true statement with regard to lifting and moving patients?

a. Your back muscles are the strongest in your body. Use them.
b. If done correctly, two properly trained EMTs should be able to lift a patient up to 600 lbs. with no additional help
c. You should keep your stomach relaxed while lifting
d. Move your body as one unit keeping the weight close to you

Question 75: You have been doing CPR on a 68 yr old male patient in VF for approximately 5 minutes when he has a Return of Spontaneous Circulation. After optimizing ventilation you notice his blood pressure is 82/50. Your protocols state to start an Epinephrine Infusion if the patient's blood pressure is below 90 systolic. You guess the patients weight in pounds is 220. According to 2010 ACLS guidelines what would be the correct dose range for an Epinephrine Infusion for this patient?

a. 22-110 mcg per minute
b. 9.9-49.5 mcg per minute
c. 50-100 mcg per minute
d. None of the above

Question 76: What range of degrees is Extreme Right Axis Deviation?

a. 0 to 90 degrees
b. 0 to -90 degrees
c. 90 to 180 degrees
d. -90 to -180 degrees

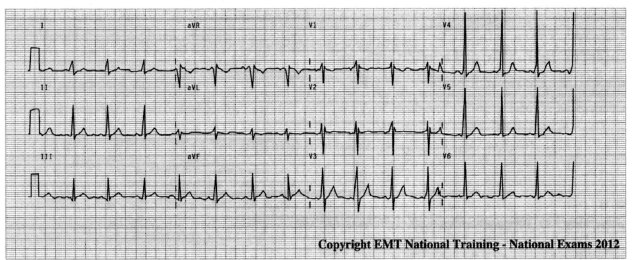

Question 77: You arrive on scene to a 73 year old male who complains of chest pain. He's alert and oriented and states he is having substernal chest discomfort radiating into his jaw. The patient denies other symptoms and states he feels fine except for the chest discomfort. Your partner takes a set of vitals and reports his blood pressure is 130/80 and oxygen saturation is 94%. You ask your partner to apply oxygen via cannula at 2LPM while you attach a 12-lead. Based on this EKG how would you treat this patient?

a. Immediately transport the patient and call an order in for a STEMI alert.

b. Continue oxygen therapy, start an IV on the patient, administer 324 ASA, 0.4mg Nitro tablet, and transport in a position of comfort.

c. Continue oxygen, start an IV on the patient, administer normal saline bolus, and transport in a position of comfort. If chest pain persists administer 3mg of Morphine.

d. The EKG is inconclusive and the most appropriate treatment is to continue oxygen therapy, start an IV, and transport the patient.

Question 78: You confirm that no pulse is present and begin CPR. Your first shock should consist of?

a. Three stacked shocks at 150 joules

b. One shock at 50 joules

c. One shock at 200 joules

d. Three stacked shocks at 120, 150, and 200 joules

Question 79: You are called to a youth summer camp for a 12 year old girl having difficulty breathing. En route to the camp you are told that a group of kids were having lunch when a hive of bees was disturbed near by. The kids took off running and when they stopped the patient began having a hard time breathing. She has no known allergies. What is the best course of action?

a. Verify low blood pressure and then administer epinephrine by auto-injector to the patient's thigh if protocols allow.

b. Ask the girl if she is choking. Initiate treatment and immediate transport in a position of comfort.

c. Apply high flow 02 at 15LPM and assess lung sounds. Place the patient in a position of comfort.

d. Confirm that the patient is not taking any new medications that may have caused the allergic reaction. Apply high flow 02 at 15LPM.

Question 80: The duration of the QRS in V1 and/or V2 must be how many seconds to diagnose a right or left bundle branch block?

a. 0.06 seconds or greater
b. 0.12 seconds or greater
c. 0.16 seconds or greater
d. 0.21 seconds or greater

Question 81: Your patient is a 3 year old girl who has attempted to ingest a penny. She is pale and has nasal flaring and intercostal retractions during inhalation that is accompanied by stridor. Her pulse is 70 and her movements are sluggish. With regard to respiratory arrest, which of the above signs is the most ominous?

a. She is sluggish
b. Her pulse is 70
c. Her skin is pale
d. Her ribs are contracting

Question 82: You are ordered by Medical Control to intubate a patient. What is the most important thing that needs to be done while you are preparing your equipment?

a. Make sure your laryngoscope is light, tight, and bright
b. Have your assistant pre-oxygenate the patient
c. Get suction ready to deal with any vomitus
d. Make sure the patient will tolerate the airway

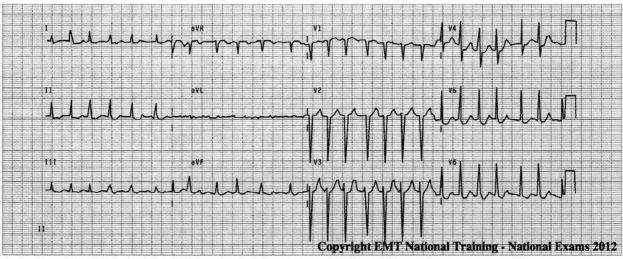

Copyright EMT National Training - National Exams 2012

Question 83: Which of the answers correctly describe this 12-lead?

a. This patient is in rapid A-fib and is currently taking cardiac medication.
b. This patient is in sinus tachycardia with inferior ischemia (II, III, aVF).
c. This patient is in SVT with ST depression in v4, v5, v6.
d. This patient has A-fib with right ventricular hypertrophy.

Question 84: Your cardiac arrest patient has a return of spontaneous circulation. The patient's blood pressure has dropped below 90 systolic and medical direction has ordered an Epinephrine infusion. What is the correct formula?

a. 1-5 mcg/kg per minute
b. .01-.05 mcg/kg per second
c. .1-.5 mcg/kg per minute
d. 10 mg over a 20 minute period

Question 85: It's 7:30 a.m. and you arrive on scene of a two car collision involving at least 6 patients on a foggy corner of a fairly busy country road. The fire department is not there yet and there is smoke and flames showing from both cars. You can hear people crying and cars are already driving around the wreckage to get past the scene. What steps should you take?

a. Begin extrication of the patients while your partner calls for more ambulances
b. Get the fire department en route, establish a safety zone and assist in keeping traffic a safe distance away
c. Triage the most critically injured first and then extricate them in order of severity
d. Inform the patients that you are not allowed by law to enter the zone until it is made safe by law enforcement

Question 86: You and your partner Bob are just pulling up to a call for a man down with CPR in progress. Dispatch has told you that the man has an extensive cardiac history and had just finished golfing with friends when he collapsed in the parking lot. According to the AHA which of the sequences is most correct?

a. Turns on AED power, Attaches AED to the patient, Check pulse and Initiate analysis of the rhythm
b. BSI, Briefly question rescuers about arrest events, Analyze rhythm, Check pulse
c. BSI, Check pulse, Begin compressions, Open airway
d. BSI, Check pulse, Open airway, Begin compressions,

Question 87: You arrive on scene to find a 50 year old male unconscious for unknown reasons. His pulse is weak and he is breathing at approximately 20 shallow breaths per minute. A blood glucose reading shows 360 mg/dL. Which of the following answer choices contains the most correct treatment?

a. Have your partner take manual c-spine stabilization, apply O2 at 10 LPM via NRB and give a 20mL/kg bolus of normal saline.
b. Begin assisting ventilations with supplemental oxygen and give 2.0 ml of glucagon via IM
c. Apply O2 at 12 LPM via NRB and administer 4 units of insulin after verifying expiration date and proper patient
d. Assist ventilations with high flow O2 and give 1 tube of oral glucose via IV

Question 88: You and your partner Duval arrive on scene to find a woman who has suffered a blunt trauma to the chest from a swing on a carnival ride. She is having difficulty breathing and upon auscultation you hear nothing on the right side. This woman likely has a_____ and would be suffering from_____as the collapsed lung is incapable of oxygenating any blood.

a. Flail chest / hyperventilation
b. Pneumothorax / hypoxia
c. Hemoptysis / hypoventilation
d. Broken jaw /severe pain

Question 89: During an assessment, a person was found to have wet lung sounds. In what position should they be transported?

a. Semi Fowler's
b. Supine
c. Trendelenburg
d. Lateral recumbent

Question 90: A child between 3-5 would have normal vitals if they were?

a. 35 breaths a minute, pulse of 88, and Systolic BP of 100
b. 24 breaths a minute, pulse of 76, and Systolic BP of 98
c. 20 breaths a minute, pulse of 120, and Systolic BP of 120
d. 20 breaths a minute, pulse of 100, and Systolic BP of 110

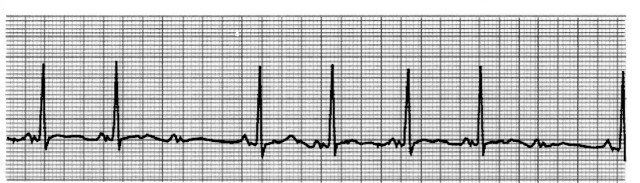

Question 91: Your patient is a 69 year male who only responds to painful stimuli by opening his eyes briefly. Your partner initiates airway management and starts an IV while you connect the monitor. The monitor shows this rhythm. What would be the next appropriate treatment?

a. Perform a rapid sequence induction
b. Initiate trans cutaneous pacing
c. Administer Epinephrine 1mg 1:10,000
d. Initiate cardioversion

Question 92: You arrive on scene to a 71 year old female with acute onset chest pain. She's pale, dyspneic, diaphoretic and denies cardiac history. Your partner applies oxygen while you attach a 4-lead with no obvious findings. Your 12-lead shows 1mm ST elevation in leads v3 and v4. What type of infarction is this patient having?

a. Inferior
b. Lateral
c. Anterior
d. Septal

Question 93: Which of the following statements regarding helicopter safety is most accurate?

a. Rotor blades may not appear to be spinning when they actually are
b. Approaching the helicopter from the up hill side is advised
c. Rotor blades may dip as low as 4 feet off the ground
d. Never allow a helicopter pilot to land where there are trees

Question 94: You arrive on scene where a 63 year old male is complaining of tenderness in the lower left side of his abdomen, fever, chills, and loss of appetite. After speaking with him you discover he has also had irregular bowel habits. Which of the following conditions causes such symptoms?

a. Diverticulitis
b. Pancreatitis
c. Cholecystitis
d. Acute Hepatitis

Question 95: You arrive on scene to find a 25-year-old woman with a red swollen eye who is complaining of pain and a burning sensation. After interview, you determine the patient accidentally splashed oven cleaner in her eye and is suffering a chemical burn to the eye. What is the best treatment for this patient?

a. Use eye dropper to clean the eye
b. Rinse each eye for 5 minutes with a hose
c. Insertion of a Morgan Lens
d. Bandage the eye and transport rapidly

Question 96: You are responding to a house fire where the report comes in that there is only one patient. He has burns that cover both of his legs. He is conscious and breathing. There are no other injuries reported. What percentage of his body is burned according to the rule of nines?

a. 27 Percent
b. 49 Percent
c. 42 Percent
d. 36 Percent

Question 97: A person who is wet _____.

a. Will be easier to defibrillate
b. Should not be defibrillated
c. Is not at risk of hypothermia
d. Is usually from drowning

Question 98: You arrive on scene to find a 78 year old man who is sitting in a chair and staring off into space. His breathing is labored and you can hear wet lung sounds. You get no response when you try to get his name. Your requests for him to move his toes go without response. He winces and withdraws slightly when his chest is rubbed. What is this patients GCS?

a. 9
b. 10
c. 11
d. 12

Question 99: Incident Command has made you transportation officer at a multiple casualty incident. A walking bridge at a nearby park has collapsed and there were 10-20 people on the bridge suffering varying degrees of injuries. You have two hospitals at your disposal. Santa Cruz Hospital is 3 miles away and Valley Hospital is 15 miles away. Which of the following transportation choices would be the BEST?

a. Send all the red tagged patients to Santa Cruz until they are at capacity. Then send any remaining red tagged patients to Valley Hospital followed by yellow and green tagged patients.
b. Send all green tagged patients to Valley Hospital first, followed by the yellow tagged patients until the hospital is at capacity. Once at capacity send all remaining patients to Santa Cruz.
c. Send all red and yellow tagged patients to Valley Hospital, and then send the green and black tagged patients to Santa Cruz Hospital.
d. Send all green tagged patients to Valley Hospital after sending all the red, yellow, and black tagged patients to Santa Cruz.

Question 100: A call comes in for a 61 yr old female with an altered LOC. When you arrive, the patient's sister tells you that the patient had a stroke about a year ago, but she knows of no other health problems. During your initial assessment, you find her eyes open and looking around. She is speaking to you, but saying inappropriate words. She will not obey your commands to "raise your arm please ma'am" and she moves her arm toward her chest when you give her a light sternal rub. What is this woman's GCS and what should you do after administering oxygen?

a. GCS of 12 / Package the patient for transport
b. GCS 7 / Get a BP, Pulse, and Respirations
c. GCS of 9 / Ask if she is taking any medications
d. GCS of 8 / Do a rapid assessment

Question 101: You are dispatched to a boat fire with multiple victims in the water. You are the only Paramedic on scene. Upon arrival you find patient #1 shivering uncontrollably, but able to answer questions appropriately. Patient #2 is on a boat across the bay with another EMS unit. That unit relates that the patient is mildly hypothermic and doesn't want to be transported. Both patients indicate that a third person was with them and that he was burned badly. On scene command confirms that this patient is still in the water. Which is the most critical patient, and why?

a. Patient #1, because she is in severe hypothermia.
b. Patient #2, because he can't reason properly.
c. Patient #3, because he will require the most care when he is removed from the water.
d. Patient #1, because she is in hypogenic shock.

Question 102: The Intrasseous route (IO) is in which category of drug administration?

a. Topical Route
b. Enteral Route
c. Parenteral Route
d. Pulmonary Route

Question 103: You and your partner Loni arrive on scene to find 4 patients. Which one of them would be your priority?

a. A 54 year old man complaining of chest pain with a BP of 130/80 and a pain severity rating of 4
b. A 17 year old with a systolic BP of 102 mm Hg
c. A 7 year old who is conscious, with respirations of 27, and a systolic of 68 mm Hg
d. A 46 year old female with a broken ankle and a broken tibia

Question 104: What would you do if a newborn infant has a heart rate lower than 100 beats a minute?

a. Ventilate at 40-60 breaths a minute
b. Begin chest compressions
c. Ventilate at 100 respirations a minute
d. None of the above

Question 105: You and your AEMT partner are dispatched to a 34 year old male with chest pain. As you approach the patient you notice he is breathing fast and holding his chest. He is able to talk to you in complete sentences and does not appear to have a diminished LOC. He states he has been under a lot of emotional stress with work and just found out his girlfriend is pregnant. He also tells you he does not have a cardiac history and feels light headed. Your partner obtains a set of vital signs while you attach a cardiac monitor. Your partner relates that the patient is breathing at 27 breaths per minute, has a blood pressure of 98/62, and a rapid pulse. Once you have the monitor attached you observe sinus tach at 175 beats a minute with a narrow QRS. After attaching oxygen and having your partner start an IV what would be the next appropriate intervention?

a. Ask the patient "to bear down" in an attempt to slow the heart rate
b. This patient is symptomatic and needs to be cardioverted immediately
c. Administer 6mg of Adenosine, rapid push followed by a 20cc flush
d. There is nothing more you can do for this patient besides rapid transport

Question 106: You arrive on scene of a 49 year old female with shortness of breath. The patients' family reports to you that she has a long standing history of COPD. You note that the patient appears to have labored breathing with audible expiratory wheezes with a respiratory rate of 36. The patient is only able to speak in 1-2 word sentences and has ashen skin color. You instruct your partner to being ventilation of this patient with a BVM. Your next course of action for this patient should be?

a. Perform a rapid trauma exam.
b. Place a PEEP valve on the BVM and ventilate the patient.
c. Perform a 12 lead EKG.
d. Discontinue BVM ventilation and administer a breathing treatment.

Question 107: If a patient has an upright QRS in Lead I and an upright QRS in Lead AVF, how would you describe their Axis Deviation

a. Right Axis Deviation
b. Left Axis Deviation
c. Normal Axis Deviation
d. Extreme Right Axis Deviation

Question 108: Cardiogenic shock could be brought on by:

a. A heart attack
b. A stroke
c. A frightening experience
d. Exposure to power cables

Question 109: Which of the following statements is true with regard to American Heart Association Advanced Cardiovascular Life Support (ACLS)?

a. ET tube drug administration is preferred to IV drug administration
b. Drugs should be delivered as soon as possible before a rhythm check
c. The provider should palpate a pulse or check the rhythm after shock delivery
d. Effective ACLS begins with high quality BLS and CPR

Question 110: The right side of the heart _____ and _____.

a. receives pulmonary circulation, drives systemic circulation
b. receives systemic circulation, drives pulmonary circulation
c. drives pulmonary circulation, drives systemic circulation
d. receives systemic circulation, receives pulmonary circulation

Question 111: You and your partner Scott are called to a trailer court for a behavioral problem. When you arrive, law enforcement is already on scene and have a man in his mid 20's handcuffed. The man is very thin and does not have a shirt on. His hair is all messed up and there is a gash on his shoulder that is still bleeding. As your partner begins treating the wound, the arresting officer tells you that a neighbor called law enforcement when the man was seen eating out of a cat food dish on the neighbor's porch. Your initial assessment shows the man has an altered LOC and will not answer any questions or make eye contact. His respiration rate appears to be normal with adequate volume and his pulse is strong and rapid at 120. His skin is pale looking and cool to the touch. What is most likely wrong with this man? How would you treat him?

a. He has a mental health issue. Dress and bandage the shoulder wound and then turn him back over to law enforcement.
b. He is hypoglycemic. Get a blood glucose reading from a fresh finger stick. Bandage the wound and administer one tube of glucose if the blood sugar reading is low.
c. He is on some sort of narcotics. Bandage the shoulder and have law enforcement assist you with moving him to the ambulance. Administer high flow O2 via NRB and transport with the patient strapped down in a supine position with ankle and wrist restraints.
d. He has a laceration on his shoulder. Apply an antiseptic to the wound and bandage it. Transport him on O2 via nasal cannula at 4 LPM.

Question 112: According to 2010 ACLS guidelines, what is the most important intervention an ACLS provider can do to improve a defibrillation attempt?

a. Endotracheal intubation
b. Chest compressions
c. Oxygen administration
d. Epinephrine administration

Question 113: Which of the following is not a way that CPAP can be applied?

a. Face mask
b. Through an ET tube
c. Nose mask
d. Through a levin tube

Question 114: A fierce winter storm has left hundreds of people stranded along a stretch of highway for a few days. You have been dispatched with the National Guard to help care for anyone suffering from exposure. As you prepare your equipment what things should you carry extra of and why?

a. Blankets; Any patients you meet will need aggressive warming and blankets are part of that
b. Drinking water; Dehydration is a very likely problem
c. Warm IV fluids; The patients will need warm IV fluids to help combat the hypothermia you will likely encounter
d. Oral glucose; If patients have not had food for a few days they may have low blood glucose levels

Question 115: Which drug and dose would be appropriate to treat rapid atrial fibrillation?

a. Adenosine 6mg
b. Diltiazem .10mg/kg
c. Midazolam 2-4mg
d. Cardizem .25mg/kg

Question 116: You are assessing a 2-month-old girl who is sleeping in her crib. Which of the following signs would cause you to be concerned?

a. Drool coming out of the child's mouth / fluttering eyelashes
b. Red cheeks and hands on the child / cries when woken from sleep
c. Difficulty waking the child up / persistent crying
d. The child crying while waking up / inability to hold head up

Question 117: You are treating a patient who is complaining of chest pain. They are diaphoretic with a blood pressure of 98/50. You have their medications on board which include a prescription for nitroglycerin. Medical control has instructed you to administer 1 nitroglycerin tablet sublingually. How would you respond?

a. Respectfully disagree and state that you feel it is in the best interest of the patient with a blood pressure so low to not lower it any further by administering nitroglycerin
b. Administer 1 nitroglycerin tablet as instructed
c. Instruct medical control to get out their protocol books and look under contraindications for nitroglycerin administration
d. Repeat the vital signs to medical control and ask if they still wish to have you administer the nitroglycerin with the blood pressure that low.

Question 118: You arrive on scene to find a 34 year old male laying on the ground in a pool of blood. Bright red blood is spurting from a large cut in his shirt sleeve and he is clutching a knife between his teeth. What should you do first?

a. Have your partner distract the patient while you take the knife from him
b. Inform the patient you will not hurt him and treat the injury
c. Call for police backup and then treat the wound
d. Leave the scene until police arrive to make the scene safe

Question 119: The immune system can over react to normally harmless foreign material. This normally harmless material is called a/n _____.

a. Antigen
b. Antagonist
c. Antiantigen
d. Protagonist

Question 120: What description below best describes Portal Hypertension?

a. Portal Hypertension is often caused in patients who take tricyclic medications, which affects only the systolic pressure.
b. Portal Hypertension can be diagnosed in pregnant women who are extremely obese, it is life threatening due to the increase in chronotropic and inotropic effects of the heart.
c. Portal Hypertension is due to liver disease commonly found in alcoholics, which can lead to a variety of disorders including ascites and esophogeal varices.
d. Portal Hypertension also called Malignant Hypertension is an acute symptom where the blood pressure rises to dangerously high levels and causes the patient to have headaches and seizures.

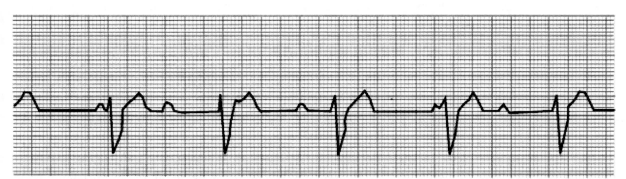

Question 121: Identify this rhythm, and which intervention would be appropriate based on the patients signs and symptoms. Patient is a 62 year old female who has been having episodes of syncope. When you arrive on scene she is not responsive when you talk to her, and moans when you give her a sternal rub. She has a history of hypertension and is currently on Propranolol. She appears to be in respiratory distress. Her BP is 88/52, and her pulse is slow and weak.

a. Second degree type I; Initiate oxygen and IV therapy and transport in a position of comfort.
b. Third Degree; Give oxygen via NRB 15L, start an IV, and immediately begin transcutaneous pacing.
c. Second Degree Type II; Give oxygen via NRB 15L, start an IV and initiate transcutaneous pacing.
d. This rhythm cannot be identified. The best course of action is to give the patient oxygen, start an IV, and immediately transport.

Question 122: What is the name of the protein that binds oxygen to the red blood cell?

a. Leukocytes
b. Erythrocytes
c. Hemoglobin
d. Plasma

Question 123: After recognition of asystole on your cardiac monitor, you should do what?

a. Confirm in a second lead
b. Administer 0.5mg Atropine
c. Continue CPR
d. Administer 1.5mg/kg of Lidocaine

Question 124: You arrive on scene to find a man in his 70's lying on his bed experiencing extreme abdominal pain. He said he has a long history of cirrhosis and alcoholism. As you are doing your physical exam you expose his abdomen to find it severely distended. What is this commonly called, and how would you treat this patient?

a. Ascites- airway management, IV, 100mcg of fentanyl, and transport in position of comfort
b. Hemorrhoids- airway management, IV, transport in position of comfort
c. Atelectasis- airway management, IV, 8mg of Zofran, transport in position of comfort
d. Gastrointestinal varices- Airway management, IV, immediate nasotracheal intubation

Question 125: BSI is a concept that considers all body tissue and body fluids as having the potential for being infectious. Who is responsible for creating this universal set of guidelines?

a. DOT
b. CDC
c. FEMA
d. All of the above

Question 126: A woman has just given birth to a healthy baby boy with the assistance of her partner. The delivery went fine, but during the delivery of the placenta she began to hemorrhage. The best course of treatment would include?

a. High flow O2 and rapid transport
b. Massage the uterus, treat for shock, and transport
c. Massage the placenta, high flow O2, and rapid transport
d. Treat for shock and apply a wet compress to the vagina

Question 127: If a patient, whom you believe is of sound mind, denies medical attention even though you know it would be in their best interest to be treated, the best thing you could do is?

a. Try to convince them again and be honest about what their condition is and the possible risks of refusal.
b. Have your partner sneak up on them and gently restrain them with hand cuffs
c. Leave the scene immediately and do not discuss the run with anyone
d. Thank them for wasting your time and have them sign a refusal of treatment form

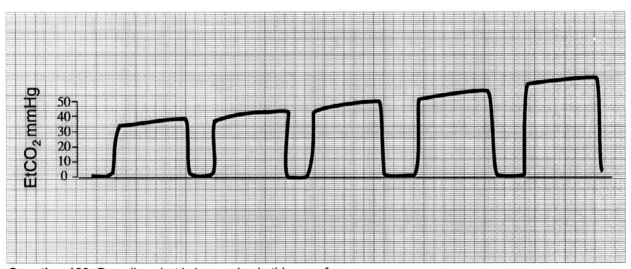

Question 128: Describe what is happening in this waveform.

a. Patient is hyperventilating
b. Patient is hypoventilating

c. Patient is being ventilated with BVM too fast

d. The patient has been moved from supine to a sitting position

Question 129: The National Incident Management System (NIMS) includes a componant referred to as "Interoperability". This componant is concerned with:

a. Inter-agency communications before, during and after an MCI.

b. The immediate establishment of Incident Command.

c. Communication between EMS, fire and law enforcement during an MCI.

d. How EMS units operate as a team when communications are down.

Question 130: You and your partner Ashley arrive at a house where dispatch reports a 911 call was made. Nobody was on the phone to report any emergency, and attempts at calling back have resulted in a busy signal. A frantic woman exits the house screaming about her daughter not breathing. You enter the home to find a 9 year old girl lying supine on the kitchen floor very cyanotic. After 2 rescue breaths, each given over a period of _____, you begin ventilations with a BVM at a rate of _____ and a tidal volume of _____.

a. 1-2 seconds / 10-12 breaths per minute / 700ml-1000ml per breath

b. 2 seconds / 12-20 breaths per minute / 800ml per breath

c. 1 second / 10-12 breaths per minute / enough air to cause adequate chest rise

d. 1 second / 12-20 breaths per minute / enough air to cause adequate chest rise

Question 131: Without any further information, what condition would you say the following patient is in? A 1-year-old male with a pulse rate of 110, breathing at 30 breaths per minute, with a systolic BP of 90.

a. Good

b. Poor

c. Bad

d. Moderate

Question 132: Using lights and sirens during a cardiac arrest transport is?

a. Mandated by the DOT

b. Not necessary

c. A consideration for moving quickly and safely through traffic

d. A good way to calm the patient

Question 133: If a patient has a negative QRS in Lead I and a negative QRS in Lead AVF, how would you describe their Axis Deviation?

a. Left Axis Deviation

b. Normal Axis Deviation

c. Right Axis Deviation

d. Extreme Right Axis Deviation

Question 134: After treating a patient in cardiac arrest you find a Return of Spontaneous Circulation, the patient's Blood Pressure has dropped below 85 systolic and medical direction has ordered Norepinephrine Infusion. What is the correct formula?

a. .1-.5 mcg/kg per minute
b. .01-.05 mcg/kg per second
c. 20-50 mg/min
d. 5-10 mcg/kg per minute

Question 135: You arrive on scene with your partner Emilio to find a woman who is having problems breathing. She is speaking in 1 or 2 word bursts and is on oxygen at 3 liters per minute. There is an ashtray next to her bed loaded with cigarette butts. She says her care taker called the ambulance and she does not want you there. She says she will allow you to take her vitals but then you have to leave. Her BP is 100/60 her pulse is 48 and her respirations are 18. She says she is 89 years old and has a pacemaker and is on high blood pressure medication. "I just want to be old, please leave", she says. What should you do?

a. Transport her to the ER. Her vitals dictate that you must
b. Tell the care giver to quit calling and giving false alarms
c. Respect her wishes and leave, asking her to please call if she needs medical attention
d. Prepare to bag her and transport when she eventually passes out

Question 136: While trying to determine why your patient is in cardiac arrest, which of the following is a correct list of reversible causes?

a. Hypoxia, Hydrogen Ion, Hypokalemia, Toxins, Thrombosis-pulmonary
b. Toxins, Tension Pneumothorax, Thyroidism, Hypokalemia, Hypothermia
c. Hyperkalemia, Hypothermia, Hypotension, Tamponade-cardiac, Thrombosis-pulmonary
d. Hypovolemia, Hydrogrn Ion, Hypoxia,Toxins, Thrombosis- cerebral,

Question 137: Continuous positive airway pressure (CPAP) is best described by which of the following definitions?

a. A tube placed through the mouth that is used to remove gastric distension.
b. Positive pressure transmitted into the airways of a patient allowing for better diffusion of gases and re-expansion of collapsed alveoli.
c. Medical procedure in which a tube is placed in the trachea via the mouth or nose.
d. A form of respiratory therapy where pressure is maintained in the airway, which results in the lungs emptying less completely in expiration.

Question 138: The process of glucose being broken down within the cell is called?

a. Biochemical process
b. Hemochemical process
c. Biodiversified process
d. Chemohemo process

Question 139: How would you appropriately treat a patient with a pulmonary embolism?

a. Continued oxygen, administer lactated ringer solution, rapid transport in a position of comfort.
b. Immediately start CPAP, administer normal saline and .25mg/kg Cartizem, rapid transport.
c. Begin ventilations with a BVM, start two IV's and start fluid resuscitation, administer Nitro, rapid transport.
d. NRB 15L/min, administer normal saline, cardioversion, rapid transport in position of comfort.

Question 140: While performing CPR on a 72 year old patient, you attempt to identify any reversible causes. Which of the following is a correct list of reversible causes?

a. Hypothermia, Hydrogen ions, Hyperthermia, Toxins, Tamponade-cardiac
b. Tension Pneumothorax, Thrombosis-coronary, Total Airway Block Hyperkalemia, Hypokalemia
c. Hypoxia, Hypovolemia, Hyperthermia, Tension Pneumothorax, Thrombosis-pulmonary
d. Toxins, Tamponade-cardiac, Thrombosis-coronary, Hypovolemia, Hypokalemia

Question 141: Which of the following are the correct dose and route for oral glucose?

a. 30g sublingual
b. 30g and swallow glucose
c. 15g buccal
d. 15g and swallow glucose

Question 142: You arrive on scene with your partner Joe to find an 7 year old boy unconscious after being dragged from the water. He is not breathing and has no pulse. CPR in this case should include_____.

a. 30:2 compression to ventilation ratio
b. 15:2 compression to ventilation ratio
c. 5:1 compression to ventilation ratio
d. 30:1 compression to ventilation ratio

Question 143: You are assisting your partner who is preparing to intubate a 79 year old woman. You are managing the BVM and begin ventilating and preoxygenating the patient at what rate?

a. 21 breaths a minute for 1 minute
b. 12-18 breaths a minute for 2-3 minutes
c. 12-20 breaths a minute for 1-2 minutes
d. 15 breaths a minute for 4 minutes

Question 144: All of the following are considered stimulants except:

a. Chloroquine
b. Amphetamine
c. Ecstasy
d. Eve

Question 145: You and your partner arrive at the home of a 59 year old male with a history of acute pulmonary edema. The patient is conscious and breathing at a rate of 28 breaths/min. Which treatment is best indicated?

a. Begin mouth-to-mask rescuscitation.
b. insert an Oropharyngeal airway
c. insert a Nasopharygeal airway
d. use a Continous Positive Airway Pressure (CPAP) device.

Question 146: A patient with heat exhaustion who is fully alert should be encouraged to?

a. Lie down with legs below the heart and ice packs to the armpits
b. Vomit up whatever is causing the problem
c. Continue sweating until they cool down
d. Sit up and slowly drink a liter of water as long as they don't feel nauseated

Question 147: You are first on scene to an MVA involving two cars. The crash scene is only blocking the south bound lane of traffic and cars from both directions are taking turns using the open north bound lane to pass the crash scene. What is your first priority?

a. To triage the patients from both cars and treat the most seriously injured first
b. To stabilize the cars and determine if airbags were deployed
c. To ensure traffic is controlled properly and the scene is safe
d. To see if a helicopter is available

Question 148: Which of the following statements best describes Axis Deviation?

a. If a patient had infarcted tissue in the left ventricle from a previous MI, It would be safe to say the patient would have Left Axis Deviation.
b. Refers to the direction of depolorization through the heart.
c. Leads II, and AVR are the best leads to use to find Axis Deviation.
d. 0 to -90 degrees is described as Extreme Right Axis Deviation

Question 149: You are on your way back from lunch when you come upon a two vehicle collision that is blocking an intersection. Both cars are engulfed in flames. What would be the best choice of action?

a. Pull the patients from the cars
b. Keep your distance until the danger is under control
c. Get the extinguisher from the ambulance
d. Radio for a Hazmat crew

Question 150: Which answer below best defines a right bundle branch block?

a. Right bundle branch is blocked and the electric impulses must find an alternate pathway to depolarize the right side of the heart
b. Electric impulses going to the left side of the heart are delayed due to a block in the designated pathway
c. Due to high blood pressure in the pulmonary arteries, the right side of the heart strains to pump efficiently and eventually fails
d. Electrical impulses are stopped by injury to the myocardium

Question 151: When treating a patient suffering from hypothermia what should you avoid doing?

a. Focused, active warming of the extremities to raise the body temperature.
b. Gentle treatment and transport to help avoid ventricular fibrillation.
c. Placing heat packs wrapped in a towel over the carotid artery and groin, per protocol.
d. Giving warm, stimulant free fluids if patient is AOX3 and is not being transported by helicopter

Question 152: Continuing with above scenario. You begin pacing and obtain electrical and mechanical capture. You reassess his vitals, blood pressure is now 96/50, respirations are 13 breaths per minute with 96% oxygen saturation. There are 2 hospitals nearby; the first hospital is 5 minutes away with a fully staffed ER. The second hospital is 20 minutes away with a fully staffed ER and cath lab. Based on your patients current condition which is the preferred hospital and what is your report?

a. Based on the patients current condition it is vital to get him to the nearest hospital so a doctor would be able to examine and stabilize him. Your report should consist of appropriate information such as: signs and symptoms, 12-lead findings, interventions done, and ETA.
b. Because your patient is having an acute myocardial infarction it is important to transport him to the hospital with the cath lab. The report should include vital signs only.
c. The patient needs to be seen by a doctor immediately. It is best to transport him to the first hospital where he can be stabilized before he is transported to a hospital with a cath lab. It would be best to focus on the patient rather than giving a report to the receiving hospital.
d. It is important to transport him to the hospital 20 minutes away with the cath lab. Your report should include signs and symptoms, 12 lead findings, interventions done, and ETA.

Question 153: AHA Guidelines specify that rescue breaths should be delivered over a period of_____.

a. 1 second
b. 2 seconds
c. 3 seconds
d. 5 seconds, 2 seconds in and 3 seconds out

Question 154: The apothecary system is for _____.

a. Estimating a child's age
b. Measuring dosage of medications
c. Breaking down hormones into usable pieces
d. Transporting combative patients

Question 155: What would you do if a new born infant does not begin spontaneously breathing after suctioning?

a. Hold the baby by its feet and give a light slap to the buttocks
b. Vigorous but gentle rubbing of the infants back
c. Begin CPR
d. Give two quick rescue breaths

Question 156: You are a paramedic treating a patient in respiratory arrest. You were able to secure an ET tube after your third attempt. Your partner notices the patient's stomach is extremely distended from your previous attempts at ventilating esophageal intubations, he orders you to insert an NG tube. What do you do?

a. Inform your partner it is contraindicated to insert an NG tube after a patient has been intubated with an ET tube.
b. Explain to your partner it is indicated to use an orogastric tube rather than an NG tube after a patient has been intubated with an ET tube.
c. You realize since the patient has been intubated you are unable to properly insert an NG tube, you immediately begin suctioning the patient's airway.
d. Make sure you have all the supplies you need and begin proper insertion of an NG tube.

Question 157: It is the middle of winter and you and your partner are called to the scene of a homeless man having breathing problems. You arrive to find him laying on a sidewalk on a calm, but very cold night. He is likely losing heat from?

a. Conduction
b. Convection
c. Refraction
d. Evaporation

Question 158: You are suctioning an unconscious patient who has vomited. It is proper procedure to suction the patient for approximately _____ and then _____.

a. 10-15 seconds / rinse the catheter in preparation of additional suctioning
b. 5-10 seconds / ventilate the patient at 12-20 breaths a minute
c. 10-15 seconds / throw the catheter tip away and put on a sterile one
d. 5-10 seconds / ventilate the patient at 100 compressions a minute

Question 159: What position should a patient be placed in to aide with the insertion of a nasogastric tube?

a. Supine
b. High Fowler's
c. Prone
d. Trendelenburg

Question 160: Your unit is called to the scene of a motor vehicle collision at a busy intersection. A man in his 40's, driving a small truck, has hit a telephone pole head on. He was unrestrained and ejected through the windshield at approximately 50 MPH. When you arrive, he has been secured to a backboard with proper c-spine precautions. His pulse is 80 beats per minute and he is breathing regularly and deeply at 12 respirations per minute. You notice that his pulse seems to weaken during inhalation. While taking his blood pressure, you see that each time he inhales, his systolic pressure drops by 20-30 mmHg. His trachea is midline and lung sounds are equal. What is the most likely reason for these vital signs?

a. Head injuries involving the pons portion of the brain often cause patients to exhibit irregular breathing patterns and irregular pulses.
b. Liquid filling the pericardium increases pressure and inhibits the ventricles from filling properly, which in turn leads to low stroke volume and low pressure
c. Air has begun filling the pleural space through a hole in the chest inhibiting the lungs from filling with air. This in turn puts pressure on the heart, causing the pressure to fluctuate with each inspiration
d. Injury to the spine may interfere with signals sent from the medulla oblongata to the diaphragm. This interference

causes a variant or irregular breathing pattern and consequent drop in blood pressure

Question 161: You are the Incident Commander at the scene of a bus rollover. A tourist group of approximately 25 senior citizens was on the bus when it overturned on a sharp corner. Which of the following actions would be appropriate?

a. Help with extrication of the patients from the bus and set up a triage area
b. Call for fire suppression from the fire department and traffic control from law enforcement, then establish a red zone
c. Assigning a triage officer, treatment officer, and a transportation officer
d. None of the actions would be appropriate

Question 162: The manner in which you must act is called?

a. Standard of practice
b. Standard of care
c. Standard of action
d. Standard of adaptation

Question 163: You are assessing an 84 year old man. Upon auscultation of the lungs you discover crackles or rale sounds. He is complaining of chest pain and congestion. These signs and symptoms can indicate?

a. An embolism
b. Collapse of the vena cava
c. Right ventricular failure
d. Left ventricular failure

Question 164: What is the most common cause of AED failure?

a. Radio interference
b. Sub freezing temperatures
c. Battery failure
d. Inappropriate shock

Question 165: A 27 year old man and his 4 year old nephew have been pulled from a river after being submerged for approximately 12 minutes. Rescue breathing for the man should include breaths at what rate? Rescue breathing for the child should include breaths at what rate?

a. 1 breath every 5-6 seconds for the man / 1 breath every 3-5 seconds for the child
b. 12-20 breaths per minute for the man / 10-12 breaths per minute for the child
c. 10-12 breaths per minute for the man / 20-30 breaths per minute for all children
d. 1 breath every 3-5 seconds for the man / 1 breath every 5-6 seconds for the child

Question 166: During endotracheal intubation of a child you should always?

a. Use a cuffed tube
b. Perform the Sellick maneuver
c. Use an uncuffed tube
d. Use the Broselow tape to ensure the correct tube is selected

Question 167: What is one very important thing to note prior to initiating CPAP therapy on a patient?

a. How much oxygen is in the tank
b. The patient's ability to walk
c. The distance of transport
d. The patient's skin color

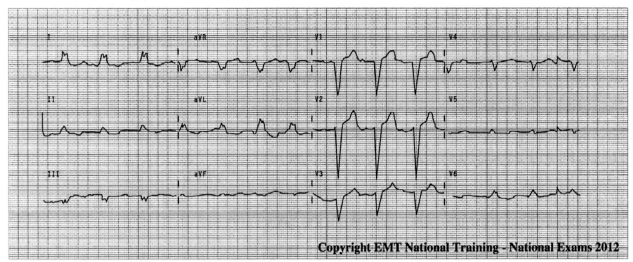

Question 168: Correctly interpret the EKG below:

a. Sinus rhythm with left bundle branch block
b. Septal Myocardial Infarction
c. Anterior Myocardial Infarction
d. Sinus Rhythm with right bundle branch block

Question 169: You are transporting a 32 year old pregnant woman who is in the 32nd week. She is complaining of stomach pain and is pale. How would you transport her?

a. Left lateral recumbent
b. Supine with feet elevated
c. Prone with a pillow under her belly
d. Modified Trendelenburg

Question 170: An ice storm has caused a 10 car pile up on a nearby interstate. Incident command has instructed you to take over triage of the patients. Patient 1 is a woman who has a broken arm and a back injury with suspected spinal cord damage. Patient 2 is male and has a broken femur and is showing signs of shock. Patient 3 is an elderly woman who has a laceration on her forehead and pain in her wrist. Patient 4 is a male, breathing at 6 breaths a minute with a head injury. What color triage tag should each of these patients receive?

a. 1Red, 2Red, 3Black, 4Red
b. 1Yellow, 2Yellow, 3Green, 4Black
c. 1Green, 2Red, 3Black, 4Red
d. 1Yellow, 2Red, 3Green, 4Red

Question 171: Most violent injuries to first responder's occur?

a. At motor vehicle accidents

b. At crime scenes

c. When a patient has a sudden behavioral change

d. In the homes of gang members

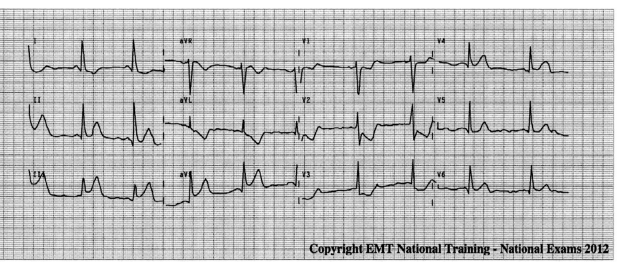

Question 172: Correctly interpret this 12-lead.

a. Inferior Myocardial Infarction with Anterior Ischemia

b. Left Bundle Branch Block with Left Axis Deviation

c. Lateral Infarction with Inferior Ischemia

d. Bi-fasicular block with Left Ventricular Hypertrophy

Question 173: You are on scene with a patient and medical control has ordred an infusion of Intropin. What drug is this?

a. Albuterol

b. Dopamine

c. Vasopressin

d. Solu-Medrol

Question 174: You are called to the scene of a woman who is having difficulty breathing. Upon arrival you notice several people surrounding the woman who seems to be agitated. Your scene assessment determines it to be safe and you approach the woman who is in the tripod position. Her breathing is rapid and shallow. She states her ribs hurt after being struck with a punch from her husband. You should?

a. Call law enforcement and leave the scene until they arrive

b. Treat the patient if the situation appears safe and inform law enforcement of the possible assault when the time is appropriate

c. Call the husband out for hitting a woman and make him look dumb in front of the rest of the family

d. Inform the woman that she will have to go to the hospital if she wants to get treated. This environment is not safe

Question 175: When the body does not have enough insulin to break down the available sugars, it begins to consume the _____ of the body.

a. Fatty acids
b. Stored fats
c. Glucose
d. Sucrose

Question 176: You and your partner Nick are dispatched to the scene of a small building fire, just as backup and possible rehabilitation. As you round a corner near the scene, you see 10-12 people lying in a yard a few houses away from the fire. Some are in obvious distress and others are walking aimlessly down the street.. Which of the following choices would be the most appropriate for you and Nick to take?

a. Do a rapid visual triage of the wounded and begin treating those with the worst injuries
b. Call dispatch and request traffic control for the street in front of the building. After law enforcement has the street secure begin triaging the patients
c. Go to the building as dispatched and report to the IC
d. Contact the IC and notify them of the current situation, triage and order more resources through command

Question 177: Your patient is a 19 year old female who is G4/P2/A1. Her boyfriend called 911 stating that the woman is a diabetic and pregnant in her third trimester. She is complaining of a headache, abdominal pain, and blurred vision. Upon arrival at the residence, you notice the woman's feet and fingers are swollen. Her pulse is 116 and her respirations are about 16 breaths per minute. The patient's blood pressure is 145/92 and auscultation of the lungs reveals rales. How many live births has this woman had? What is most likely wrong with her and how should she be treated? Choose the best answer.

a. She has had 2 live births. She has preeclampsia and should be transported to the hospital in a left lateral position while on high flow O2. Initiate an IV line TKO if protocols and scope of practice allow.
b. She has had 4 live births. She has placenta previa or abruptio and should be transported in a left lateral recumbent position while administering O2 and IV therapy TKO if scope of practice allows
c. She has had 2 live births. She has eclampsia and should be transported in a position of comfort while administering high flow oxygen and IV therapy if your scope of practice allows.
d. She has had 1 live birth. She has supine hypotensive syndrome and should be put on a backboard and rapidly transported to the ER while on high flow O2. IV therapy should be initiated, if within scope of practice and local protocols.

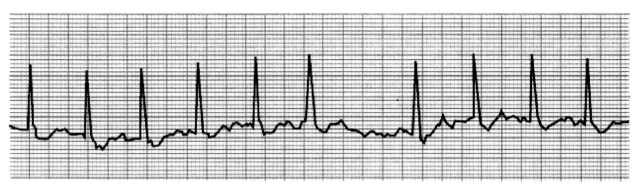

Question 178: If you are preparing to perform synchronized cardioversion with this patient, what is the correct setting to start with?

a. 50J
b. 100J
c. 120J

Copyright 2013 EMT-National-Training

d. 150J

Question 179: You have just drawn blood from a woman who protested the whole time telling you to stop. You have just?

a. Got to draw blood from some patients
b. About had it with her
c. Committed assault
d. Committed battery

Question 180: You are called to the scene of a structure fire. Upon arrival you notice several people staggering down the block away from the fire with soot marks around their mouths. You should?

a. Tell them to stay where they are and wait until you come back
b. Call for additional ambulances and continue to assess the scene
c. Treat them immediately and find out if there are others in the building
d. Get ready for the building to explode because it could be a meth lab

Question 181: You arrive on scene to find a situation that is too hazardous to enter. What should the EMT do to help ensure that the scene is not entered by unauthorized personnel?

a. Create a safety perimeter to help keep people away from the scene
b. Stay near the scene in your ambulance in order to maintain crowd control
c. Get on the loud speaker and tell everyone to stay back or they will be arrested
d. All of the above

Question 182: Place the following steps in order for accessing a non tunneled, tunneled, and peripherally inserted CVAD:
1. Explain the procedure to the patient, clamp the catheter, and wipe the site with povidone-iodine and let dry.
2. Replace the clamp, remove syringe, connect the IV tubing to the catheter, and ensure no air is present in tubing.
3. Connect the syringe, unclamp the catheter, and draw 5 mL of blood.
4. Prepare equipment, draw 3-5mL normal saline, and put on gloves.
5. Replace the clamp, attach the syringe of normal saline to the catheter, remove the clamp and flush.
6. Remove clamp, begin infusion, tape the connection site, and administer fluid and drugs.

a. 1,4,3,5,2,6
b. 4,1,5,3,2,6
c. 4,1,3,5,2,6
d. 1,4,5,3,2,6

Question 183: Which of the following steps are not helpful in preventing complications of vascular access devices?

a. Ensuring the correct medication, dose, and nutrition is being infused into the device
b. Not placing a blood pressure cuff on an arm containing a device port
c. Ensuring the patient is in semi fowler's position
d. Carefully examining the device before any treatment

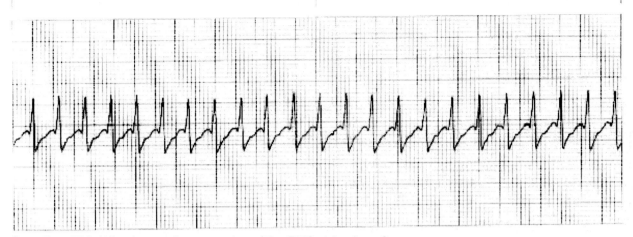

Question 184: What is your interpretation of the EKG strip above?

a. Junctional Tachycardia
b. Sinus Tachycardia
c. Supraventricular Tachycardia (SVT)
d. Sinus Tachycardia with PVC's

Question 185: Which of the following is not a complication of a central venous catheter placed in a child?

a. Dislodged or broken catheter
b. Obstruction
c. Slow infusion
d. Infection

Question 186: You arrive on scene with your partner Steve to a Mexican restaurant where someone called in to report a choking. You enter to find a mid 30's female laying supine on the floor. She is cyanotic and unconscious. Her family says she had just taken a bite of Chimichanga when she began choking and eventually fell to the floor. What are you going to do?

a. Verify dyspnea, give two slow breaths with high flow O2, and back thrusts
b. Head tilt chin lift, verify apnea, two slow breaths, compressions, magill forceps, and laryngoscope
c. Abdominal thrusts, finger sweep, and high flow O2
d. Ask the bystanders what happened, verify no pulse, attach AED, tell everyone to stand back, and hit analyze

Question 187: The umbilical cord is wrapped tightly around the baby's neck and you have tried unsuccessfully to slip the cord over the head. What should your next course of action be?

a. Push the baby's head into the vagina until the cord comes loose
b. Clamp the cord in two places and cut it in the middle
c. Support the head and suction the baby's nose and mouth
d. Massage the uterus to stimulate harder contractions to free the baby

Question 188: When interpreting a 12-lead how do you correctly diagnose left ventricular hypertrophy?

a. If you see a large R wave in v1 that becomes progressively smaller from v2, to v3, to v4, the patient has left ventricular hypertrophy.

b. Add v1's S wave in mm and the R wave in v5, if the total is greater than or equal to 35 mm the patient has left ventricular hypertrophy.

c. Add v4's R wave in mm of the R wave in v5, if the total is equal or greater than 25 mm, the patient has left ventricular hypertrophy.

d. If the R wave in v3 becomes progressively longer throughout v4, v5, and v6 your patient has left ventricular hypertrophy.

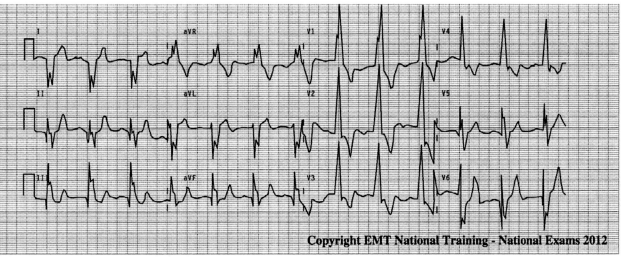

Question 189: Correctly interpret this rhythm.

a. Sinus rhythm, poor R progression, Right Bundle Branch Block with Right Axis Deviation

b. Sinus rhythm, wide QRS, Left Bundle Branch Block with Left Axis Deviation

c. Sinus Arythmia, with global ST depression, and Left Bundle Branch Block

d. Acclerated ventricualr rhythm, Right Bundle Branch Block with anterior fasicular block

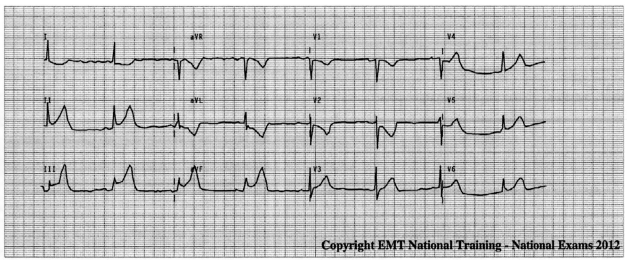

Question 190: You and your EMT partner are dispatched to a residence of a 42-year-old male with a chief complaint of chest discomfort. When you arrive on scene you see a thin male who appears to be in relatively good shape sitting comfortably in his chair holding his chest. He tells you he is training for a marathon and just got back from running 13 miles about 30 minutes ago. While doing his cool down stretches he suddenly felt chest discomfort in the center of his chest that started radiating down his left arm. He rates the discomfort a 3 out of 10 and states he has never felt this type of discomfort before. He describes it as a dull feeling. He goes on to tell you he has been in the Olympics twice for

long-distance running and tells you he is now training for the next Olympics. He states his normal heart rate is in the low 50s and has no other symptoms other than the chest discomfort. Your partner takes a baseline set of vitals and tells you his blood pressure is 110/70 and the patient is breathing 16 bpm and oxygen saturation is 98% on room air. You attach a 12-lead and hit analyze, the monitor prints this strip. What is the correct interpretation of the 12-lead?

a. Inferior MI
b. Lateral MI
c. Anterior MI
d. The 12-lead is inconclusive

Question 191: How many compressions per minute would you give an adult patient who has no pulse?

a. 80-100 compressions per minute
b. 100-120 compressions per minute
c. 60-80 compressions per minute
d. 30-2 compressions per minute

Question 192: Place the following steps in order for inserting a nasogastric tube: (1) Confirm placement by auscultating the epigastrum. (2) Correctly measure from nose to ear and ear to xiphoid process. (3) Place the tube into the largest nostril and adjust to the appropriate length. (4) After attaching suction, lubricate the distal end for insertion. (5) Insert the tube down the midline into the oropharynx. (6) Inject 80-100 mL of air into the NG tube. (7) Have the patient tilt their head forward and swallow as the tube is being inserted.

a. 2,7,5,1
b. 4,2,3,6
c. 2,4,3,1
d. 4,5,1,6

Question 193: Where is a central venous catheter placed on a child?

a. Antecubital vein
b. Large central vein such as the subclavian
c. Great saphenous vein
d. Large arteries such as the Aorta

Question 194: Which of the following is a shockable rhythm?

a. VT
b. AT
c. Asystole
d. PEA

Question 195: You arrive on scene to find a 5-year-old child whose central venous catheter has broken, resulting in leaking fluid. What should be done for this patient?

a. Assess the patient and transport
b. Immediately disconnect the catheter
c. Use a sterile technique to clamp off the broken line
d. Put 4x4's and pressure over the site and transport

Question 196: A tanker truck carrying unknown chemicals has overturned on the interstate and a bright fluid is reported leaking from the truck's trailer. Several injuries are reported and many bystanders are reportedly vomiting. IC has given you the responsibility of setting up a helicopter landing zone. Which of the following potential areas would be the most appropriate for this zone?

a. A slight slope approximately 80 feet X 80 feet that is uphill and upwind of the hazardous incident
b. A flat hard surface downhill and at least 100 meters away from the hazardous incident
c. A flat hill top at least 1 mile from the hazardous incident and downwind of any part of the scene
d. A football field directly adjacent to the scene that was evacuated after reports of vomiting

Question 197: Which of the following is not used for airway maintenance and ventilation?

a. OPA
b. NPA
c. BVM
d. DAP

Question 198: Hypothermia is diagnosed when the body's organs are below what temperature?

a. 92 degrees
b. 96 degrees
c. 95 degrees
d. 98.6 degrees

Question 199: You arrive on scene to find a 35 year-old-male complaining of a burning pain in the left upper quadrant, vomiting blood, and melena. Which of the following is the likely cause of these symptoms?

a. Appendicitis
b. Diverticulitis
c. Ulcerative Colitis
d. Peptic Ulcer Disease

Question 200: An explosion has occurred at a nearby petroleum refinery. Incident Command has appointed you as the triage officer. What color triage tag would each of the following patients receive? Patient 1 is a 9 year old female with a broken arm. She is breathing at 8 breaths a minute. Patient 2 is an elderly male with a compound fracture of the left femur. He is in decompensated shock from loss of blood and has no pulse. Patient 3 is an elderly man who has a laceration on his forehead and a GCS of 8. Patient 4 is a 5 year old male breathing at 18 breaths a minute with a head contusion.

a. 1Red, 2Red, 3Yellow, 4Yellow
b. 1Red, 2Black, 3Red, 4Green
c. 1Yellow, 2Red, 3Black, 4Red
d. 1Red, 2Red, 3Yellow, 4Yellow

Question 201: Where is a non-tunneled CVAD inserted?

a. Into the small intestine
b. Into the gallbladder
c. Into the antecubital vein (AC)
d. Through the skin into the subclavian vein

Question 202: Poor R wave progression on a 12-lead can be caused by all of the following except?

a. Myocardial Ischemia
b. Anterior Myocardial Infarction
c. Left Bundle Branch Block
d. Wolff-Parkinson-White Syndrome

Question 203: You and your partner Pepe arrive on scene to find a man in his early twenties with a large gash on his forearm that is spurting blood. You immediately apply pressure with your gloved hand as Pepe hands you a trauma dressing. The patient is pale with a weak rapid pulse and respirations of 30 breaths per minute. As you are finishing your initial assessment and bandaging the wound the PT tells you to "get away" from him. Your best course of action would be to do what?

a. Have Pepe wrestle him onto the stretcher.
b. Explain to the patient that you are almost finished bandaging his wound and you will leave him alone then
c. Stop bandaging the wound and call for police assistance in restraining the patient for transport
d. Tell the patient you cannot leave him until the wound is bandaged and then restrain him to the stretcher

Question 204: You and your partner Toby arrive at a motel in response to a 911 call for an unconscious female. You find the woman pulseless and while Toby hooks up the AED, you begin delivering compressions. How many compressions per minute would you give this woman?

a. 60-80 compressions per minute
b. 100-109 compressions per minute
c. 150 compressions per minute
d. 90-100 compressions per minute

Question 205: History and assessment findings for hypoglycemia may include of all of the following except:

a. polyuria
b. bizarre behavior
c. coma late in episode
d. hunger

Question 206: You have requested helicopter transportation of a critical burn patient. The remote nature of the accident will force the helicopter to land on an incline. From which direction should you approach the helicopter?

a. The back
b. The front
c. The uphill side
d. The downhill side

Question 207: You arrive on scene to a 62 year old male with chief complaint of hematemesis. The patient is sitting on the couch with a large bucket in front of him violently vomiting bright red blood. You take the appropriate BSI precautions and ask the patient when this began. He explains he has been an alcoholic for 30 years and this happens from time to time. What is this patient most likely suffering from, and how would you treat him?

a. Pancreatitis- place a nasogastric tube in the patient and start fluid administration, transport.
b. Crohn's Disease- Treat patient by placing in a position of comfort and gentle transport to the hospital.
c. Gastroenteritis- Insert a nasogastric tube, start an IV and begin fluid administration, transport.

d. Esophageal Varices- Ensure the patient continues to have an airway, start an IV, begin a fluid resuscitation, transport.

Question 208: You are dispatched to an accident involving two semi trucks and several cars that have collided under an overpass. The reporting party says that there are several people in the road and nobody is helping them. Your unit is the first to arrive on scene. After performing a thorough scene size-up, what should you do?

a. Triage the patients
b. Call for more ambulances
c. Assume command of the scene
d. Establish a safety officer

Question 209: The 2010 ACLS guidelines recommend the temperature of the fluid used when inducing hypothermia during post-cardiac arrest care to be?

a. 5 degrees Celsius
b. 4 Degrees Celsius
c. 3 Degrees Celsius
d. 2 Degrees Celsius

Question 210: You arrive on scene to find a 22 year old male complaining of intense lower right quadrant abdominal cramping. Upon further examination you discover that prior to the severe cramping he had slight cramping, nausea, vomiting, a fever. Which of the following condtions is most likely the cause?

a. Crohn's Disease
b. Hemorrhoids
c. Appendicitis
d. Acute Hepatitis

Question 211: When transmitting a number with two or more digits you should say the whole number first, followed by:

a. Saying it again
b. Saying each number individually
c. Saying, "Do you copy?"
d. Saying it in Spanish

Question 212: A woman's obstetrical history can be displayed using P and G. How would you display a woman's history who has had 3 pregnancies and 2 live births?

a. P-3 - G-2
b. P3G-2
c. G3P3
d. G3P2

Question 213: Medical control is responsible for all of the following EXCEPT:

a. Overseeing patient care
b. Making decisions about proper patient care
c. Getting the patient to the hospital safely and quickly
d. Ensuring use of common protocols

Question 214: What disease is caused from abnormally high levels of corticosteroid hormones produced by the adrenal glands? It can cause increased facial hair, weight gain, muscle atrophy, and a moon face appearence.

a. Addison Disease
b. Myxedema
c. Grave Disease
d. Cushing Syndrome

Question 215: You arrive on scene to find a 26-year-old male with a red, swollen eye who is complaining of pain and a scratching feeling. After interviewing him, he believes a piece of metal flew into his eye while he was grinding metal. What is the best treatment for the patient?

a. Rinse the eye with lactated ringer's solution
b. Insertion of a Morgan Lens
c. Bandage the eye and transport
d. Rinse the eye with normal saline solution

Question 216: When is an infant considered premature?

a. It is born before the 37th week of pregnancy
b. It is born before the 32nd week of pregnancy
c. It is born before the 36th week of pregnancy
d. All of the above

Question 217: It's 4:30 p.m., you and your partner Jim are called to a motor vehicle accident on a busy side street. You arrive on scene and can see at least 6 patients from 4 cars. The cars are a twisted mess and are covering one whole lane of traffic with multiple fluids pooling around the cars. You can hear people crying and traffic is already starting to move around and by the wreck. You should...?

a. Immediately have a helicopter dispatched, begin extrication of the patients while your partner calls for more ambulances
b. Assure the fire department is en route, establish a safety zone, and assist in keeping traffic at a safe distance
c. Triage the most critically injured first after dealing with the pools of liquids
d. Notify the injured people that you are not allowed by law to enter the zone until it is made safe by law enforcement

Question 218: You arrive on scene to find a woman in her 20's who phoned in her own diabetic emergency. She is now unconscious and breathing at 20 a minute with a pulse of 110. She told the dispatcher on the phone that she had hypoglycemia and had not eaten that day. Your best course of treatment would include?

a. A ham sandwich and soda
b. 1-2 tubes of glucose orally until she feels better
c. ARGAD if accessible
d. Obtain a blood sugar, O2 via NRB at 15 lpm, and Initiate an IV of D5W

Question 219: What is the area of hazardous contamination known as?

a. Green zone
b. Yellow zone
c. Hot zone
d. Black zone

Question 220: You arrive on scene to find a 57 year old man who is sitting on a couch appearing to stare at the wall. His breathing is labored and you can hear wet breath sounds that are producing a pink foam dripping from his mouth. You get no response when you try to get his name. Your requests for him to move his arm go without response. His pulse is 105 and his BP is 92/40. You do not see any edema, swelling, or JVD. This patient likely has _____.

a. Left sided CHF
b. Hypoglycemia
c. Right sided CHF
d. Appendicitis

Question 221: Pancuronium is classified as what type of medication?

a. Alpha 2 stimulant
b. Beta 1 antagonist
c. Benzodiazepine
d. Non-depolarizing neuromuscular blocker

Question 222: A 26 year old woman has called the ambulance because she has begun delivery of her baby. Dispatch says the mother stated the baby's foot was sticking out of the vaginal opening. You should be prepared to?

a. High flow 02 on the mother, rapid transport, and gently maneuver the baby's foot back into the vagina
b. Place patient into a knee to chest position and rapid transport
c. Ask the mother to push and assist with the rest of the delivery
d. Gently pull the rest of the baby out by the foot sticking out

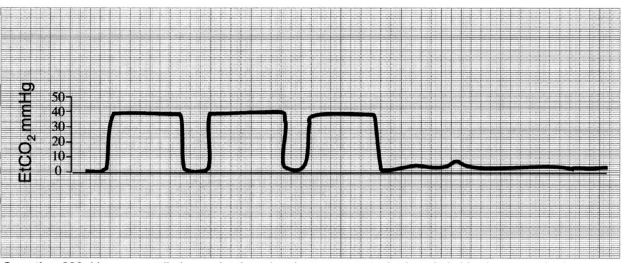

Question 223: You are ventilating an intubated patient en route to the hospital. You have attached capnography and after a few minutes notice this waveform. What is the first thing you should do?

a. Nothing, this is normal, continue ventilating the patient
b. Immediately check for pulse
c. Increase ventilations per minute
d. Check placement of ET tube

Question 224: You arrive on scene to find a 25 year old female complaining of fatigue, rectal bleeding, and nausea. After evaluating her you discover she has also had bloody diarrhea and a fever. Which of the following conditions would cause these symptoms?

a. Ulcerative Colitis
b. Mallory-Weiss Syndrome
c. Acute Gastroenteritis
d. Pancreatitis

Question 225: Which solution has the same osmotic pressure as the fluids in the human body?

a. Isotonic
b. Hypertonic
c. Hypotonic
d. Colonic

Question 226: When would a nasogastric tube be used over an orogastric tube?

a. In an unconscious patient without a gag reflex
b. In a patient with severe facial trauma
c. In a conscious patient with severe nausea
d. In a conscious patient with airway occlusion

Question 227: According to AHA CPR and AED guidelines, a patient with a VF rhythm should be shocked how many times before CPR is resumed?

a. 1
b. 2
c. 3
d. 4

Question 228: Assessment findings and symptoms for a patient that has taken a hallucinogen include all of the following except:

a. Intensified vision
b. Lacrimation
c. Tachycardia
d. Hypertensive

Question 229: You arrive on scene of a one-car motor vehicle accident. A single female patient can be observed in the car having breathing difficulties. You notice power lines are down across the hood of the car but you do not see any sparks. What would be your best course of action?

a. Get the patient extricated as quickly as possible
b. Notify the power company and keep a safe distance until they have removed the wires
c. Provide assisted ventilations while maintaining c-spine
d. Avoid the wires and begin assessing the patient

Question 230: You arrive on scene of a 54 year old female with 8 out of 10 chest pain. She denies cardiac history and reports the pain started while cooking dinner. She describes the pain as dull and non-radiating. Your partner obtains a baseline set of vitals while you perform a 12 lead ECG. You notice 2mm ST elevation in leads II, III, and aVF. What type of infarction is this patient having?

a. Septal Infarction
b. Anterior Infarction
c. Inferior Infarction
d. Lateral Infarction

Question 231: You arrive on scene for a possible poisoning. The patient is a 9 month old girl who was found with an open bottle of drain cleaner. She has a bump on her forehead and is noticeably irritable. During your assessment you note that the child does not make eye contact with you at all. Which of the following is the best course of action and why?

a. Initiate transport with blow by oxygen. The lack of eye contact and irritability are concerning signs in children this age.
b. Administer activated charcoal based on the child's weight. Diluting the poison now will help the child vomit thus eliminating much of the poison.
c. Administer O2 via nasal cannula and check the child's pupils for reactivity. The bump on the head may be the real issue.
d. Encourage the parents to immediately transport the child to their pediatrician for evaluation. A pediatrician is better trained to deal with pediatric emergencies.

Question 232: What usually happens to the ventricles of the heart when Adenosine is administered to a patient for SVT?

a. It excites the purkinje fibers causing the ventricles to beat at a faster pace
b. It has a chronotropic affect causing the ventricles to beat harder
c. It does not affect the ventricles, Adenosine only affects the atrium
d. It causes ventricular asystole for a short period of time

Question 233: Your patient is an 8 year old girl who fell from a swing and hit her head. She has a pulse but is not breathing. Your CPR should include what?

a. Breaths at a rate of 12-20
b. Breaths at a rate of 10-12
c. Breaths at a rate of 20-30
d. Chest compressions and ventilations at a ratio of 30:2

Question 234: When using waveform capnography during post-cardiac arrest care you will ventilate the patient to achieve a PETCO2 reading of_____mm Hg?

a. 20-30
b. 0-10
c. 25-35
d. 35-40

Question 235: How many beats a minute would constitute bradycardia in a school-aged child?

a. More than 80
b. Less than 70
c. More than 90
d. Less than 90

Question 236: You are performing CPR on a man in cardiac arrest. Which of the following choices would you administer first?

a. Vasopressin 20 units
b. Atropine 1mg
c. Epinephrine (1:1000) 1mg
d. Vasopressin 40 units Vasopressin 40 units

Question 237: You connect a 4-lead EKG to a patient and observe sinus bradycardia. You decide to administer Atropine per protocol. What is the maximum dose of Atropine you can administer to a patient?

a. 3mg
b. 1.5mg
c. .5mg
d. 2mg

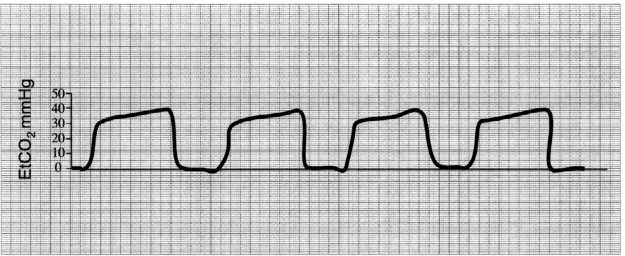

Question 238: Your partner is ventilating a patient with a BVM after return of spontaneous circulation. You have this waveform showing on your monitor. What are your instructions to your partner regarding the ventilation rate.

a. Increase ventilations
b. Decrease ventilations
c. Continue same ventilation rate
d. Re-check ET tube placement

Question 239: You have been called to a home where a 1-year-old girl is in respiratory distress, possible apnea. The caregiver called 911 after finding the girl on the floor in front of the T.V. She does not know if the child is breathing or not. Which of the following choices below contains the most accurate facts related to this call?

a. Children have a large tongue that takes up more of the oropharynx and can cause an airway obstruction. Proper administration of CPR should include about an inch of padding under the child's shoulders.
b. Children may have anterior displacement of the tongue which can cause an airway obstruction. CPR should include delicate compressions to avoid rib fractures.
c. Children have ridged tracheal cartilage and a short epiglottis that can easily block the airway. During CPR the neck should be slightly hyperextended to account for this difference.
d. Children have smaller airways that are often blocked by toys and rarely occluded with mucus or swelling. If you suspect a foreign body airway obstruction, try to visually locate the object and remove it if possible.

Question 240: You arrive on scene to an MVA involving 1 car with 3 passengers. Which of the following signs would most increase your suspicion that the driver may have significant internal injuries?

a. The passenger in the front is dead.
b. The car is wrapped around a tree.
c. The roads are icy and the speed limit is 60 MPH.
d. The driver has an altered level of consciousness.

Question 241: According to the American Heart Association what is the first alternative if intravenous access fails?

a. Intramuscular Route
b. External Jugular Route
c. Intraosseous Route
d. Endotracheal Route

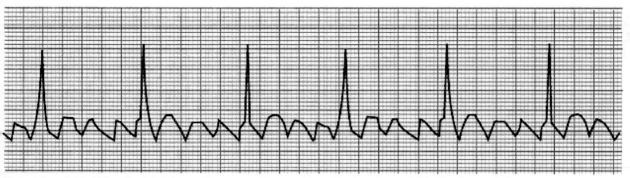

Question 242: What is the correct interpretation and conduction rate of this rhythm strip?

a. A-fib, 3:1 conduction
b. A-flutter - 3:1 conduction
c. Bradycardic Dysrhythmia - 4:1 conduction
d. Junctional Rhythm - 1:4 conduction

Question 243: A man has burns all over his head as well as over his entire genitalia, but nowhere else on his body. What percentage of the man's body is burned according to the rule of nines?

a. 9 Percent
b. 10 Percent
c. 18 Percent
d. 27 Percent

Question 244: What is the best description of how Adenosine affects the heart?

a. Blocks electrical activity in the AV node
b. Acts as a Calcium Channel Blocker and slows the conduction of the AV node
c. Acts as a parasympatholytic and inhibits actions of acetycholine receptor sites
d. Stimulates both Alpha and Beta receptors

Question 245: You arrive on scene to find a female patient actively having contractions every 10-12 minutes apart. A visual inspection of the patient reveals no visible crowning. Which stage of labor would you consider this patient to be in?

a. 1st stage of labor.
b. 2nd stage of labor.
c. 3rd stage of labor
d. 4th stage of labor

Question 246: What is the generic name for Versed?

a. Lorazepam
b. Midazolam
c. Diazepam
d. Alprazolam

Question 247: A patient with pulmonary edema that presents with shortness of breath and crackles would best benefit from which of the following?

a. Continuous positive airway pressure
b. Endotracheal intubation
c. Duoneb treatment
d. Positive end expiratory pressure

Question 248: You are dispatched to the scene of an unconscious woman. Upon arrival you are confronted by a 35 year old man who is very upset and appears to have the mental capacity of a 10 year old. He takes you by the hand and leads you into the bedroom where his mother, a woman in her 70s is sitting in a chair unresponsive. The man wants to know if his mother is ok and why she won't speak. You should?

a. Tell the man you are going to take care of his mother and that he may ride in the ambulance with her to the hospital
b. Tell the man to calm down so you can help his mother. If he continues his agitation have him restrained
c. Explain to the man that his mother is very sick and if you don't get her to the hospital she will die
d. Tell him that his mom will be fine and to wait for a call from hospital administration

Question 249: Stimulation of alpha receptors will likely?

a. Drop blood pressure
b. Dilate blood vessels
c. Constrict blood vessels
d. Cause the patient to become hypotensive

Question 250: You arrive on scene to a patient who has been having seizures for over 3 minutes. You have been ordered to start an IV and administer 2mg of Lorazepam. What drug are you going to give?

a. Versed
b. Ativan
c. Morphine
d. Valium

Answers

Question 1: You arrive on scene to a patient with chest pain and shortness of breath. Her son tells you she started having chest pain four hours ago and has not been acting normal for the past hour. He also tells you she has had a history of CHF and some heart problems. You attach a monitor and observe this rhythm. She is also breathing approximately 26 bpm, and has a blood pressure of 81/50. Based on this description, what would be the most appropriate treatment for this patient?

a. Cardioversion beginning at 120

Rationale: The rhythm shows A-fib; based on signs and symptoms, the best intervention for this patient would be cardioversion. Something to ask yourself when you are presented with these types of scenario questions are, "Is the person presenting sick or not sick (symptommatic or nonsymptommatic)? Do they have an altered LOC, hypotensive, breathing issues, extreme heart rate changes, etc?" If the person is presenting as sick they will need more aggressive treatment. If they are presenting with symptoms but not as serious, they will probably need something less evasive. These types of scenario questions will be on the NREMT exam and you will need to know based on their signs and symptoms which intervention is best.

Question 2: You are on scene of a motor vehicle accident where the car has left the road and collided with a group of trees. The driver was alone and is out of the car standing on the road. You see that the airbag on the driver's side has deployed. Which of the following recommendations would be best to follow?

c. Lift the airbag away from the steering wheel and look for damage to the steering column and wheel.

Rationale: The best recommendation is to inspect the steering wheel for damage that may be hidden by the deployed airbag. Damage to the wheel would increase your suspicion that the driver had internal injuries sustained from contact with the wheel. While a standing take down may be warranted based on assessment, it should not be a rapid take down. Detaching the battery cables is recommended when extricating passengers from a vehicle where the airbag/s have not deployed. In this case the only passenger was out of the car making detaching the cables pointless. You would not have a patient lay down to complete a spinal assessment; this may exacerbate any injury he or she has. Do your assessment with the patient standing up and use the standing takedown technique if you suspect spinal trauma.

Question 3: Giving a patient nitroglycerin during a cardiac emergency will?

c. Dilate the vessels

Rationale: Vasodilation is the desired effect of nitroglycerin, helping reduce the workload on the heart.

Question 4: If someone has audible inspiratory stridor they may have _____.

b. An upper airway obstruction

Rationale: Stridor on inspiration suggests a person has an upper airway obstruction and has a life threatening problem. Stridor on exhalation suggests a lower airway restriction.

Question 5: You and your partner Amber arrive on scene to find a pregnant woman in her 38th week. She feels like she is in active labor and requests transport to the hospital. While your partner takes vital signs in route you are assessing how far along the delivery is. You see the patient has some hemorrhaging from the vagina which leads you to believe she may have_____ or _____ and that she should be transported on her _____.

d. Placenta previa or placenta abruptio / left side

Rationale: Placenta abruptio is when the placenta prematurely separates from the wall of the uterus and placenta previa is when the placenta is blocking the cervix and presenting before the baby. They are best managed by transporting the patient on her left side to prevent supine hypotension.

Question 6: You respond to a call of a man down in a very rough neighborhood. Upon entering the location of the call you notice a group of young men in a fist fight at what appears to be the address of the call. There are two men on the ground not moving and your lights and sirens have frightened the other men away. What should you do next?

a. Call for police to secure the scene and wait for them to arrive

Rationale: As much as you want to help the injured you must be sure the scene is safe first and you cannot do that without police help in this instance.

Question 7: After doing CPR on a 72 yr old female patient in VF for over 6 minutes she suddenly has a Return of Spontaneous Circulation. After optimizing ventilation you notice her blood pressure is 79/50. Your protocols state to start a Norepinephrine Infusion if the patients blood pressure is below 90 systolic. You guess the patients weight in pounds is 90. According to 2010 ACLS guidelines what would be the correct dose range for a Norepinephrine Infusion for this patient?

d. 4.05-20.25 mcg/kg per minute

Rationale: According to 2010 ACLS guidelines the formula for a Norepinephrine Infusion for post cardiac arrest care is .1-.5 mcg/kg per minute. If the patient weighs 90 pounds you would need to convert his weight to kilograms. This is done by dividing his weight by 2 and subtracting 10%. Example: 90/2=45-10%=40.5kg. An easy way to find 10% of a number is move the decimal to the left once (45.=4.5....45-4.5=40.5). Now that you have the patients weight in kg you can figure out the dose (40.5x.1=4.05 and 40.5x.5=20.25 mcg/kg). All ACLS drug formulas could be asked on the NREMT exam, so it would be in your best interest to know them.

Question 8: The Incident Command System (ICS) is used to:

a. Ensure efficient use of resources, public and responder safety, as well as the successful completion of incident management goals.

Rationale: The primary focus of the Incident Command System is to establish a well organized, safe, efficiently managed incident scene. It can be used on a simple call involving only 1 responding unit or a call that uses hundreds of resources and involves multiple agencies.

Question 9: You and your partner Wilson arrive on scene to a fire that is under control. You are treating a patient with full thickness burns to the arm. During transport to the helicopter Wilson says, "Hey, what zone of the burn is the part that will recover?" You respond, "The _____.

d. Zone of hyperemia

Rationale: Zone of coagulation is the central part of the burn. Zone of stasis has partial viable tissue out from that. Then there is the zone of hyperemia which is the part that will most likely recover from the injury.

Question 10: Medications can be administered through a number of different routes. Which answer choice is NOT one of them?

a. Interstitial

Rationale: Interstitial is not a route of medication administration.

Question 11: You arrive on scene to find a 62 year old female in cardiac arrest. The fire department has already initiated CPR and attached an AED. You quickly assess the patient for reversible causes. According to the 2010 ACLS guidelines which of the following T's below is not a reversible cause?

b. Thrombosis-cerebral

Rationale: According to the 2010 ACLS guidelines Thrombosis-cerebral is not a reversible cause. The T's are Tension Pneumothorax, Tamponade-cardiac, Toxins, Thrombosis-coronary, and Thrombosis-pulmonary. The H's to look for are Hypovolemia, Hypoxia, Hydrogen ion (acidosis), Hypo/Hyperkalemia, and Hypothermia.

Question 12: You arrive on scene with your partner Jermain to assist on a mass casualty. You have just begun tending an arterial bleed on a woman who was thrown from a car when you hear the cries of a baby. You have the woman maintain pressure on the bleed with a trauma dressing and go to the car with the infant crying. What did you just do?

a. Abandon a patient

Rationale: Abandonment is that action of leaving a patient without an equal or more advanced level of care to replace you. The Good Samaritan Law will not protect you in the instances of negligence, abandonment, or any other instance where you are not acting in the best interest of a patient.

Question 13: You respond to a patient who is short of breath. Upon arrival, you encounter a 54 year old patient who is conscious, alert to your presence and appears oriented. The patient is Diaphoretic and in apparent respiratory distress. She is seated in the tripod position with pursed lips. Your initial treatment consists of high flow oxygen and a baseline set of vitals. Your next course of treatment should include the following?

d. CPAP with duo-neb treatment

Rationale: The best possible treatment for this patient would be to apply CPAP and place an inline duo-neb treatment based on her current presentation. Since the patient is still spontaneously breathing along with her being oriented, she would respond best with CPAP to increase lung compliance. A duo-neb set up with albuterol and atrovent would help with bronchodilation and prevent the drying up of any secretions.

Question 14: You and your partner Janell are just approaching the scene of a two vehicle collision. One of the vehicles is on it's side and the distinct smell of propane can be detected. A high pitch whistling sound can be heard from the overturned vehicle and you can see the driver has been partially ejected through the window. Janell calls for Hazmat as you:

b. Ensure that the ambulance is parked a safe distance from the scene

Rationale: Scene safety is priority 1 and making sure the ambulance is parked at a safe distance is the only appropriate answer. Flares may cause an explosion or fire. You would not enter the scene or do triage until Hazmat has made the scene safe.

Question 15: You assess a patient who you believe is not acting rationally. They have an altered LOC and a large gash on the side of their head that is actively bleeding. The patient is adamantly refusing treatment. Which would be the best course of action?

b. Contact medical control and request police assistance in managing the patient

Rationale: If you believe they are not behaving rationally because of the injury and could potentially be a danger to others or themselves, you should call medical control and get police assistance in getting the patient to definitive care.

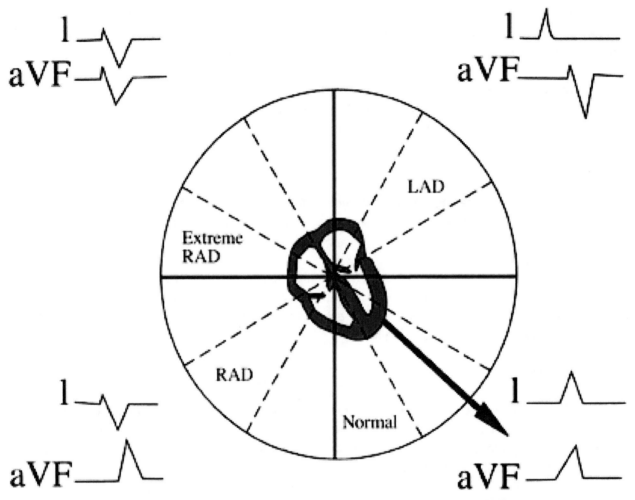

Question 16: If a patient has a positive QRS in Lead I and a negative QRS in Lead AVF, how would you describe their Axis Deviation?

b. Left Axis Deviation

Rationale: If a patient had a positive QRS in lead I and a negative QRS in AVF, this would indicate a Left Axis Deviation.

Question 17: You are setting up the landing zone for a helicopter transport of a critical MVA patient. Which of the following would be considered acceptable methods of marking the boundaries of this zone?

c. 4 vehicles with their lights pointed inward

Rationale: Things like tape, garbage cans, flares, and sheets can easily become airborne with the force of a rotor blade coming down on them and should not be used. Vehicles in an X is acceptable and often used for night landings.

Question 18: According to the 2010 AHA guidelines, how many shocks should be delivered prior to resuming CPR?

a. 1 shock

Rationale: According to the 2010 AHA guidelines, if the single shock does not convert the rhythm, cerebral and coronary perfusion must be initiated.

Question 19: After performing CPR on a 62 year old patient in cardiac arrest, your patient has a return of spontaneous circulation. At what rate are you going to tell your partner to ventilate the patient?

a. Start ventilating the patient at a rate of 10-12 breaths a minute and titrate to achieve a PETCO2 of 35-40mm Hg.

Rationale: 2010 ACLS guidelines state that after the patient has a Return Of Spontaneous Circulation, you should begin ventilating the patient at 10-12 breaths per minute and titrate to achieve a PETCO2 of 35-40mm Hg to avoid excessive ventilation.

Question 20: What is a contraindication for the use of CPAP?

a. A patient with nausea/vomiting

Rationale: A patient who is vomiting or likely to vomit is not a candidate for CPAP therapy. A tight fitting mask seal increases the risk of aspiration of vomitus. Fatigued patients talking in short sentences may not adequately communicate the need to vomit and are often too tired to remove the mask rapidly. You must always monitor a patient closely after you apply the CPAP mask.

Question 21: A 6 year old girl was found outside in her yard unconscious. She is breathing 6 breaths a minute and her pulse is 58 bpm with poor systematic perfusion. What should you do?

b. Initiate chest compressions and assist ventilations with high flow O2

Rationale: AHA Guidelines for BLS include compressions for children with a pulse rate of less than 60 bpm who are perfusing poorly. Symptomatic bradycardia is a common terminal rhythm in infants and children. Don't wait for pulseless arrest to begin compressions.

Question 22: You come upon a victim of asphyxial cardiac arrest. Which of the following is the correct order of action?

c. Do CPR for 5 cycles or approximately 2 minutes and then activate the emergency response system and retrieve the AED

Rationale: AHA CPR Guidelines specify that treatment for asphyxial cardiac arrest should begin with 5 cycles of CPR prior to activating the emergency response system or retrieving the AED.

Question 23: Your patient is an unresponsive 44 year old female who has a pulse but is not breathing. How should you proceed with CPR?

b. 2 quick rescue breaths and then provide 10-12 breaths per minute

Rationale: AHA guidelines state that If she has a pulse, you only want to provide ventilatory support with 2 rescue breaths and 10-12 breaths per minute.

Question 24: What would be an expected systolic BP in infants, toddlers, and preschool aged children?

d. 80 mm Hg

Rationale: Infant 70-90, toddler 70-100, and preschool 80-110.

Question 25: Baroreceptors are sensory nerve endings that _____.

b. Sense changes in blood pressure

Rationale: Baroreceptors sense changes in BP from vasoconstriction and vasodilation.

Question 26: What are two contraindications for the use of a Combitube?

d. The patient is under 4ft tall/You know they have esophageal disease

Rationale: The only two that truly are contraindications are the patient height and known disease of the esophagus.

Question 27: A freight car has overturned and is spilling hundreds of gallons of hazardous chemicals into a local creek. Incident Command has told you that the toxicity of the hazardous material is a level 3. What level of protection must any personnel entering this area be wearing?

d. Level A or B protection

Rationale: Toxicity level 3 is very hazardous and thus requires a high level of protection. Level A or B protection is required in this case. Toxicity goes from 0 to 4, with 4 being the worst and 0 being little or no threat. Protection level goes from A to D. A being the highest level of protection and D being the lowest level of protection.

Question 28: You and your partner Bill arrive on scene to a head on collision involving 2 cars. After making sure the scene was safe, your partner moves to the first car to open the patient's airway. What technique should Bill use to do this?

d. Jaw thrust

Rationale: Because of the trauma, you would use the least invasive of the opening maneuvers, which is the jaw thrust.

Question 29: In a 3rd degree heart block the P R interval will be?

d. Variant

Rationale: Since the block at the AV node is complete, none of the atrial impulses are conducted through to the ventricles.

Question 30: You arrive on scene to a 63 year old male with chest pain. The patient reports acute onset, 8-10, and crushing substernal chest pain which he rates 8 out of 10. The patient is pale, cool, diaphoretic, and short of breath. He reports onset of symptoms 20 minutes ago while watching TV. He denies any cardiac history. The patient is breathing 22 times a minute and has an oxygen saturation of 92%. Your partner reports a blood pressure of 110/55. You have your partner apply oxygen, while you obtain a 12-lead. Which of the following answers below is the correct ECG interpretation?

d. Lateral Ischemia

Rationale: Based on the patients signs, symptoms and the 12-lead, the patient is having ischemia in the left lateral portion of his heart. You can see 1-2mm ST depression in leads v5 and v6. You also can see at least .5mm ST depression in leads aVL and I. These leads all look at the lateral portion of the heart. If the patient was having anterior ischemia you would see ST depression in leads v3 and v4. If the person was having an inferior or septal infarction you would see ST elevation of .5mm or greater not ST depression.

Question 31: The incident commander has put you in control of a night time medivac of a cardiac arrest patient. Which of the following would be considered appropriate?

a. Secure all equipment and supplies that could become airborne

Rationale: Securing all equipment and supplies that could become airborne is the only appropriate answer. The landing zone should be a minimum of 60 feet by 60 feet but preferred to be at 100 X 100. You do not want to shine any lights into the air while the helicopter is landing. A big X made out of rocks would not likely be visible at night from the helicopter.

Question 32: An ambulance unit or fire department that makes an uncoordinated, independent decision during an incident is said to be:

d. Freelancing

Rationale: Any individual, unit, or agency that is making decisions outside of the ICS system is considered to be freelancing. This type of behavior can lead to chaos, injury, and even death. It is vital that all responders at a scene understand the role of Incident Command and follow the direction of the Incident Commander.

Question 33: Which of the following is true of BiPAP?

c. BiPAP is a leak tolerant system

Rationale: BiPAP is a leak tolerant system while CPAP is not. BiPAP provides two levels of pressure, a higher pressure during inhalation and a lesser pressure during exhalation. BiPAP is similar to CPAP when the patient inhales not exhales. BiPAP combines partial ventilatory support and CPAP, not PEEP.

Question 34: Which of the following combines partial ventilatory support and CPAP?

d. Biphasic positive airway pressure

Rationale: Biphasic positive airway pressure (BiPAP) combines partial ventilatory support and CPAP. BiPAP involves two different types of pressure. The inhalation is similar to CPAP and the exhalation involves a drop of pressure, which eases breathing. Endotracheal intubation is placing an ETT in the trachea. PEEP is positive end expiratory pressure. A Venturi mask allows for ambient air to mix with the oxygen the mask delivers.

Question 35: You are called to a neighborhood pool where a 5 year old girl was found floating unconscious. She is cyanotic and has no muscle tone. Your partner Greg does not find a pulse and the child is not breathing. Your CPR should include a compression to ventilation ratio of_____ and each compression should be at a depth of_____.

b. 15:2 / one third of the anterior-posterior diameter of the chest

Rationale: 2010 AHA CPR Guidelines specify that 2 person CPR by health care professionals should be done at a 15:2 ratio. Each chest compression should be 1/3 of the anterior-posterior diameter of the chest. These numbers are argued by more EMT AND Paramedic candidates than any other question type we have. Please refer to your 2010 AHA CPR for Healthcare Provider guidelines.

Question 36: You arrive on scene of a 62 year old male with acute onset of chest pain. The patient states he was walking down his driveway to get the mail when his chest begin to hurt. The origin of the pain is substernal and it is radiating to his jaw and down his left arm. You tell your partner to take vitals and you attach the monitor. You print the four lead and immediately notice 3mm ST elevation in lead II. From this information what do you immediately know?

d. You do not have enough information to make an informed decision

Rationale: Based on the 4-lead, you can not know what is happening with this patient. To make a field impression of an MI you need ST elevation in 2 or more contiguous leads. A 12 lead ECG is the gold standard for identifying infarction in the pre-hospital setting. If the Patient was ischemic you would see ST depression, and you cannot tell if the patient has a right bundle branch block from lead II. Remember just because you see ST elevation in one lead does not mean the patient is having an MI.

Question 37: Incident Command has put you in charge of setting up the landing zone for a helicopter transport. What size area will you try to procure for this zone? What is the minimum acceptable size for this zone?

b. 100 feet X 100 feet / minimum of 60 feet X 60 feet

Rationale: 100 feet by 100 feet square is the preferred size of a helicopter landing zone at night. It should not be smaller than 60 feet by 60 feet during the day.

Question 38: You are dispatched to a cardiac arrest. Your patient is a 56 year old female who collapsed at a funeral. Upon arrival your EMT partner begins CPR while you hook up the monitor and start an IV in the left AC. After 2 minutes of CPR you stop and check the patient's rhythm and note that she is in v-fib. You deliver 1 shock and your partner immediately continues CPR. After 30 seconds you then administer 1mg of Epinephrine. Your partner finishes 5 cycles of CPR and you check the monitor and see a sinus rhythm. What is the next step you should take?

c. Check the patient's pulse

Rationale: According to 2010 ACLS guidelines, the very next step is to see if the patient has a pulse, you want to confirm the patient is not in PEA, if the patient was in PEA than you would want to continue CPR. If there were a pulse you would want to start ROSC protocol. Make sure you have your ACLS Algorithms memorized to the very detail. You will see these in your practical and written exams for NREMT. Know your stuff...

Question 39: All of the following are considered stimulants except:

c. Diazepam

Rationale: Stimulants produce an excited state and include: amphetamine, methamphetamine, phentermine hydrochloride, ecstasy, eve, cocaine, and PCP

Question 40: A train derailment has caused two tanker cars to explode and several others to begin leaking an unknown gas. The size of the affected area is large and crosses several county lines. According to NIMS, this type of MCI would benefit most from a:

b. Unified Command System

Rationale: Unified Command Systems can involve many different agencies such as EMS, Fire Departments, Law Enforcment, City Managers, County Commisioners, etc.

Question 41: When administering oxygen to a patient with COPD experiencing diffuse chest pain and shortness of breath, you should?

b. You do not administer oxygen any differently than you would to any other patient

Rationale: For the average person, the trigger that respirations and/or perfusion is inadequate is an increase of CO_2 in the cerebral spinal fluid. In the COPD patient it is increased O_2. You should never withhold oxygen from a patient with this

Question 42: You and your partner Maria have just started CPR on a 23 year old MVA victim. According to AHA CPR guidelines how often should you change compressor roles?

b. Every 2 minutes

Rationale: AHA CPR Guidelines say to change compressor roles every 2 minutes. Studies have shown that the quality of CPR compressions typically diminish after two minutes.

Question 43: An Incident Command System is designed to:

d. Manage and control emergency responders and resources

Rationale: Incident Command Systems are utilized to manage resources and responders and are very useful in mass casualty events and scenes that contain hazardous materials.

Question 44: You are called to a scene of a 3-year-old who is not breathing and is pulseless. Your CPR should include compressions at what depth?

c. At least 1/3rd the depth of the chest

Rationale: 2010 AHA guidelines stipulate that at least 1/3rd of the anterior posterior diameter of the chest should be compressed while performing CPR on a child.

Question 45: You are the first EMS unit on scene of a multiple casualty incident. A crane has fallen from a building roof top and ripped through an adjacent building. What should you do according to the ICS?

d. Take incident command until relieved or reassigned

Rationale: If you are the first EMS personnel on scene you should inform dispatch that you are the IC until notified differently. Once other personnel arrive on scene, you may be reassigned to triage, transportation, treatment, or logistics.

Question 46: The structure of an incident command system:

b. Can contain multiple sectors, but only one incident commander

Rationale: The structure of an ICS can be broken down into several different sectors from EMS, Fire, Hazmat, Extrication etc. Different officers may be appointed to lead each sector of the operation. It is very effective.

Question 47: What is the proper sequence of intubating a patient?

d. Check equipment, insert tube, remove laryngoscope, and inflate cuff

Rationale: Although there are steps missing in between some of the main steps, the best answer is, check your equipment, insert tube, and remove laryngoscope. All the other choices are out of order.

Question 48: An adult with a respiration rate of _____per minute would be considered within normal limits. A child aged 3-5 with a respiration rate of_____per minute would be considered within normal limits and an infant who is breathing at_____per minute would be considered within normal limits.

d. 16, 25, 40

Rationale: According to NES guidelines normal adult respiratory rates are from 16-20 - preschool aged children (3-5)children are 20-30 and infants are 40-60 initially and drop to 30-40 after a few minutes.

Question 49: You are called to treat a 69 year old male who has fallen and lost consciousness. He has a laceration on his head and is breathing very rapidly. Which of the following is a likely cause?

d. All of the above

Rationale: Any of these answers have the potential for being the cause of someone to lose consciousness. It may be medical, it may be physical.

Question 50: You and your partner have been called by law enforcement to a residence for an apparent case of physical child abuse. Upon entering the dwelling you see a 3 or 4-year-old boy sitting with a female officer. During assessment you notice bruising on the child's stomach and chest. The child says he fell off the trampoline. What is your primary concern on this scene?

d. Recognizing the potential for internal injuries based on the bruises located on the child's stomach and chest.

Rationale: It is extremely important to remember that any force that is strong enough to leave bruising on a child's chest and abdomen is strong enough to have caused internal injuries to the vital organ systems that are housed in those two body spaces. In addition, you should perform a full head-to-toe assessment of the patient to determine if any other injuries exist. Your job is not to determine if abuse occurred, but to treat the injuries you find. If the child actually fell off the trampoline, that impact is enough mechanism of injury to warrant your concern and a detailed assessment.

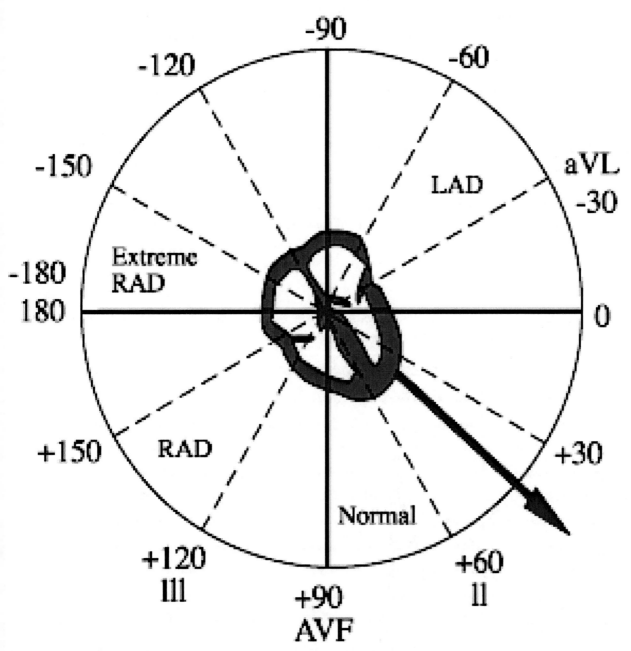

Question 51: What range of degrees is Left Axis Deviation?

a. 0 to -90 degrees

Rationale: 0 to 90 degrees is Normal Deviation, 90 to 180 degrees is Right Axis Deviation, 0 to -90 is Left Axis Deviation, -90 to -180 is Extreme Right Axis Deviation.

Question 52: After treating a patient in cardiac arrest the patient has a return of spontaneous circulation (ROSC). The patients blood pressure is below 80 systolic and you prepare to begin a Dopamine infusion. What is the correct formula?

b. 5-10 mcg/kg per minute

Rationale: 2010 ACLS guidelines state that after ROSC if the patients BP is below 90 a vasopressor infusion of Dopamine, Epinepherine, or Norepinepherine would be in order based on protocol. A Dopamine infusion is 5-10 mcg/kg per minute. It is important to know any drug calculation from the ACLS guidelines could be asked on your NREMT exam, so know your formulas.

Question 53: Your patient is a 65 year old male with chest pain. As you attach the cardiac monitor he becomes unresponsive and pulseless. Your cardiac monitor shows ventricular fibrillation. According to 2010 ACLS guidelines what is the correct sequence of steps to follow when treating this patient?

b. Began CPR, defibrillate when monitor is ready, continue CPR 30:2, 40 units of vasopressin

Rationale: If you witness a patient go into V-fib, ACLS states you can defibrillate without doing a full 2 minutes of CPR. You would want to initiate CPR until the defibrillation pads are on and the monitor is ready. You can then stop CPR, deliver a shock, then continue CPR. You may also substitute vasopressin for epinepherine for the first or second dose.

Question 54: Your patient is a 74 year old female who had an episode of syncope. You attach a cardiac monitor, note sinus bradycardia, and make the decision to administer Atropine. If multiple doses are needed, how long do you need to wait between each dose?

b. 3-5 minutes

Rationale: According to 2010 ACLS guidelines, the dosage for Atropine is .5mg every 3-5 minutes, for a maximum dosage of 3mg. Every drug in ACLS and PALS can be used in the NREMT exams. Know your stuff!!!

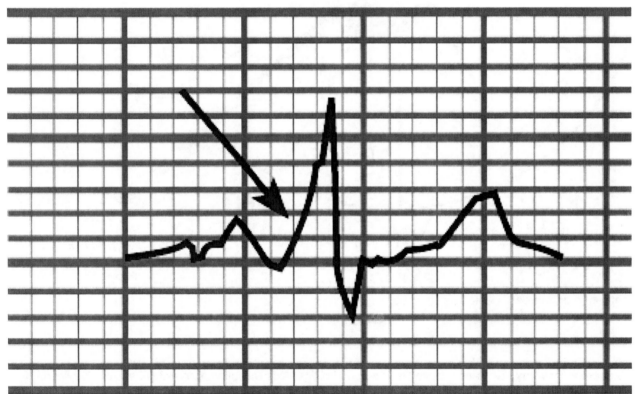

Question 55: Which of the following answers below would help you identify that a patient has Wolff-Parkinson-White Syndrome?

d. Consistent rhythm of Delta Waves.

Rationale: Classic signs of Wolff-Parkinson-White syndrome are Delta waves, short P-R interval, and QRS widening. As seen in the picture below there is a shortened P-R interval and a slurred upstroke, this is called a Delta wave. You do not need a 12 lead to identify WPW. People with WPW are susceptible to paroxysmal SVT, but just because a patient is suffering from paroxysmal SVT does not mean they have WPW.

Question 56: You arrive on scene to a patient that has a history of anxiety. She has not been taking her medications as prescribed. As you look at her medication list you notice she is prescribed Diazepam, what drug is this commonly known as?

c. Valium

Rationale: Diazepam is the generic name for Valium. Alprazolam is the generic name for Xanax. Lorazepam is the generic name for Ativan. Midazolam is the generic name for Versed. You will notice that all of the generic names end with "am" this is a common theme with benzodiazepines. Versed, Ativan, and Valium are common benzo's used in EMS. Valium depresses the limbic, thalamic, and hypothalamic regions of the CNS. In EMS it can be indicated for seizures, anxiety, pre-sedation for cardioversion, and alcohol withdrawals.

Question 57: You arrive on scene to a find 2 EMT's performing CPR on a 76 year old male in cardiac arrest. You attach the cardiac monitor and began assessing the patient for reversible causes. According to the 2010 ACLS guidelines which of the following H's is not a reversible cause?

a. Hyperthermia

Rationale: According to the 2010 ACLS guidelines Hyperthermia is not a reversible cause, the H's to look for are Hypovolemia, Hypoxia, Hydrogen ion (acidosis), Hypo/Hyperkalemia, Hypothermia. The T's are as follows Tension Pneumothorax, Tamponade-cardiac, Toxins, Thrombosis-pulmonary, and Thrombosis-coronary.

Question 58: You arrive on scene to a 71 year old male with shortness of breath and chest pain. He informs you he has a history of A-fib and is prescribed Warfarin but has not taken it in the last 3 days and has no history of respiratory problems. When you take his vitals you notice he is breathing at a rate of 26 per minute, SPO2 is 89%, he is tachycardic with an irregular rhythm and is hypotensive. You administer oxygen and start an IV. When you reassess his vitals after 5 minutes you notice the patient has not improved and his SPO2 reading has dropped to 87%. Based on this information what might be happening to this patient?

d. Pulmonary Embolism

Rationale: The signs and symptoms above would put this patient at risk for a pulmonary embolism. If a patient has rapid A-fib and is on blood thinners (Warfarin) but stops taking them, he's at risk for a clot. Unexplained shortness of breath, tachycardia and hypotension are also signs of PE.

Question 59: Your patient is an 86 year old woman who states she is feeling "funny and light headed." As you are talking with her she becomes unresponsive and apneic. What should you immediately do?

d. Assess her pulse

Rationale: You would immediately want to assess her pulse to see if she has gone into cardiac arrest and to know if CPR needs to be started. 2010 AHA guidelines place a priority on CAB instead of ABC as in the past. If the patient had a pulse, you would immediately begin to provide ventilatory support. If the patient were pulseless you would start compressions and then provide 2 ventilations after the first 30 compressions.

Question 60: One pupil dilated and the other constricted would suggest what type of injury?

b. Cerebral

Rationale: Unequal pupils are associated with head trauma and cerebral hemorrhage.

Question 61: Your patient is a 14 year old girl who is complaining of vaginal pain after falling onto the center post of her bike. She is alone and very scared. She has called the accident in on her cell phone and stated that she is bleeding very badly and feeling faint. Besides treating for shock, what other things should you consider with this patient?

d. Having a female EMT respond for the patient's modesty

Rationale: Having a female EMT respond out of concern for the patient's modesty would be a good consideration. Unfortunately, having a female EMT is not always possible.

Question 62: In which 2 leads on a 12 lead can you commonly identify a Left Bundle Branch Block (LBBB)?

b. Leads V5, V6

Rationale: LBBB can be identified in leads V5 and V6, and also in V1 and V2.

Question 63: You arrive on scene to a 74 year old who is having a COPD exacerbation. You have about a 45 minute transport to the hospital. As part of your treatment, medical direction has ordered you to administer Methylprednisolone, what is this drug commonly known as?

b. Solu-Medrol

Rationale: Solu-Medrol is the brand name for Methylprednisolone, Proventil is the brand name for Albuterol, Atrovent is the brand name for Ipatropium, and Terbutaline is a generic name for Brethine. Solu-Medrol suppresses the immune system, it can be used for anaphylaxsis, asthma/COPD, and has shown to be effective in spinal cord injuries

Question 64: A postictal state can be accompanied by deep rapid breathing that is meant to burn off excess C02 in the body. This state, prior to the elimination of CO2, could be referred to as?

d. Respiratory acidosis

Rationale: Respiratory acidosis is the buildup of CO2 in the blood as a result of a poor respiratory function. The breathing is meant to rid the blood of CO2 at a faster rate.

Question 65: Typically atrial fibrillation will present with a tachycardic response when observing an EKG. Which prescribed medication slows the rate of A-fib?

c. Digoxin

Rationale: Digoxin is a cardiac glycoside that controls the rate of a-fib and aflutter. This is important for a paramedic to know because a person prescribed Digoxin has a known arrhythmia. It is also important to know since the administration of calcium channel blockers with digoxin can cause an increase in serum digoxin levels and when administered with beta-blockers, can cause severe bradycardia.

Question 66: HIPAA stands for _____.

d. Health insurance portability and accountability act

Rationale: Health insurance portability and accountability act is a law relating to privacy in the EMS system.

Question 67: You arrive on scene with your partner Wayne to find a man at a bowling alley in respiratory distress. He is walking around looking pale and acting agitated. Audible wheezing sounds can be heard as he breathes in. His cousin says he was just getting ready to bowl when he started coughing and now it's like this. You ask the man if he is choking and he wheezes "yes". What should you do for this patient?

c. Transport and encourage him to cough

Rationale: Until there is a complete blockage of air, you do not want to give the Heimlich maneuver. Best treatment would be encouraging to cough and transport to the hospital.

Question 68: When treating hypotension during return of spontaneous circulation (ROSC) following cardiac arrest, how much and what type of IV bolus does the 2010 ACLS guidelines recommend?

d. 1-2L Normal Saline

Rationale: 2010 ACLS guidelines recommend 1-2L Normal Saline or Lactated Ringer's infusion during ROSC in a hypotensive patient . (Systolic B/P less than 90). Hypothermic protocol specifies the fluid to be at 4 degrees Celsius if the patient is unable to follow commands.

Question 69: Indications of CPAP would include all of the following except?

d. Unable to tolerate mask

Rationale: If the patient is not able to tolerate the mask with CPAP, it is contraindicated for use. This is due to the potential for the patient to become more anxious. When this occurs, it causes an increase in the patients' respiratory rate and thus, exacerbating their condition and ultimately sending them into respiratory arrest.

Question 70: Your patient is a 44 year old male who appears to be having an allergic reaction to shrimp. He is pale and diaphoretic with diffuse erythema and urticaria on his trunk. He has his own Epipen, but has not used it. His pulse is 100 and his BP is 90/50. He states he is taking 40mg of nebivolol a day. He also tells you that he is beginning to have difficulty swallowing. Which of the following would be the best treatment and why?

b. Administer epinephrine and prepare to give an additional dosage. Patients taking nebivolol may require more epinephrine.

Rationale: Regardless of whether you know what nebivolol is or does, the correct answer is to administer epi and prepare to give more. Nebivolol is a beta blocker that relaxes the arteries in order to reduce blood pressure. When you give epi it constricts the vasculature, which is working against the effects of the beta blocker. Because of this, it is likely to take more epi to get the desired effect of maintaining an open airway and increasing the blood pressure.

Question 71: You are called to a boat launch at Lake Santa Cruz for a 36-year-old female who has fallen and injured her leg. You arrive to find a female patient with extreme pain in the left thigh. She is lying on the dock screaming while several people who are drinking beer offer their advice. You direct your team to apply a traction splint because you find:

c. Palpable deformity mid-shaft in the injured femur

Rationale: Traction splints are used primarily to secure fractures of the shaft of the femur, which are usually identified by pain, swelling, and deformity of the mid-thigh or mid-shaft area of the femur.

Question 72: You and your partner Gertrude arrive on scene to find two men who have been in a fist fight and have been handcuffed by police. You have been asked to treat both men. While Gertrude is treating one man for facial lacerations and a contusion on the head, the man begins to have a seizure. What would you do?

b. Make sure your patient was in equal or more advanced care and then assist Gertrude with airway management

Rationale: You must make sure your patient has equal or better care before leaving, or else it constitutes abandonment.

Question 73: You have been unsuccessful in starting an IV on a 2 year old child that is in cardiac arrest. Your medical direction indicates you should consider initiating IO access to administer medications. As you prepare this procedure what are the anatomical landmarks you are looking for, and what are the complication risks with this procedure?

b. proximal tibia / pulmonary embolism

Rationale: The proximal tibia is the usual site to establish an IO catheter in a pediatric patient. All of the above mentioned complication risks are correct. Fracture of the tibia, pulmonary embolism, compartment syndrome, and severe pain upon infusion of fluids can be possible when initiating IO access.

Question 74: Which of the following is a true statement with regard to lifting and moving patients?

d. Move your body as one unit keeping the weight close to you

Rationale: The only correct answer is to move your body as a single unit keeping the weight of the patient/stretcher close to you. You should keep your stomach tight and use your legs, NOT your back. If you have any question of your ability to safely move the patient, get additional help.

Question 75: You have been doing CPR on a 68 yr old male patient in VF for approximately 5 minutes when he has a Return of Spontaneous Circulation. After optimizing ventilation you notice his blood pressure is 82/50. Your protocols state to start an Epinephrine Infusion if the patient's blood pressure is below 90 systolic. You guess the patients weight in pounds is 220. According to 2010 ACLS guidelines what would be the correct dose range for an Epinephrine Infusion for this patient?

b. 9.9-49.5 mcg per minute

Rationale: According to 2010 ACLS guidelines the formula for an Epinephrine Infusion for post cardiac arrest care is .1-.5 mcg/kg per minute. If the patient weighs 220 pounds you would need to convert his weight to kilograms, you do this by dividing his weight by 2 and subtracting 10%. 220/2=110-10%=99kg. An easy way to find 10% of a number is move the decimal to the left once (110.=11.0....110-11=99). Now that you have the patients weight in kg you can figure out the dose (99x.1=9.9 and 99x.5=49.5 mcg/kg). All ACLS drug formulas could be asked on the NREMT exam, so it would be in your best interest to know them.

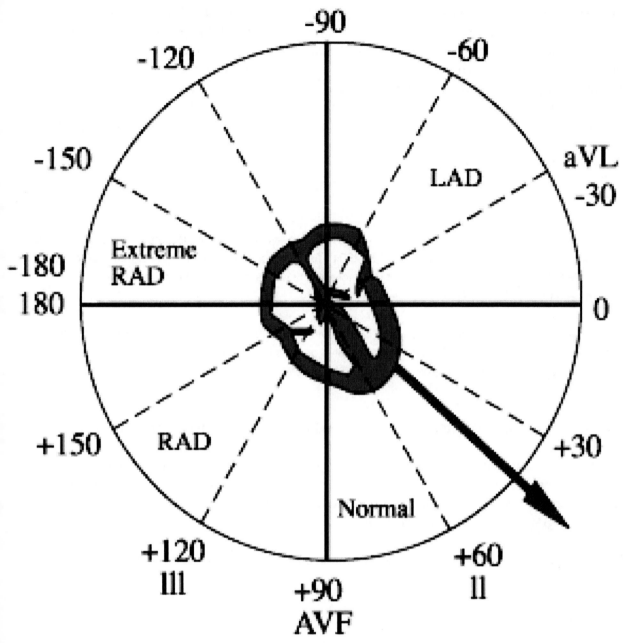

Question 76: What range of degrees is Extreme Right Axis Deviation?

d. -90 to -180 degrees

Rationale: 0 to 90 degrees is Normal Deviation, 90 to 180 degrees is Right Axis Deviation, 0 to -90 is Left Axis Deviation, -90 to -180 is Extreme Right Axis Deviation.

Question 77: You arrive on scene to a 73 year old male who complains of chest pain. He's alert and oriented and states he is having substernal chest discomfort radiating into his jaw. The patient denies other symptoms and states he feels fine except for the chest discomfort. Your partner takes a set of vitals and reports his blood pressure is 130/80 and oxygen saturation is 94%. You ask your partner to apply oxygen via cannula at 2LPM while you attach a 12-lead. Based on this EKG how would you treat this patient?

b. Continue oxygen therapy, start an IV on the patient, administer 324 ASA, 0.4mg Nitro tablet, and transport in a position of comfort.

Copyright 2013 EMT-National-Training

Rationale: The EKG above shows a patient in a normal sinus rhythm at approximately 80bpm with no other remarkable findings. At this point you would want to treat the patient according to ACS protocol, which is IV, oxygen, ASA, Nitro, and transport to the hospital. You continue monitoring the patient and administer up to 3 Nitro tablets if his blood pressure stays above 90 systolic and he continues to have chest pain. If after the 3 nitro tablets the patient continues to have chest pain, you could administer morphine. In order to call in a STEMI alert you need to see ST elevation of over 1mm or more in 2 or more precordial or adjacent leads. The last two answers are inappropriate, you should treat your patient according to the 2010 ACLS ACS protocols. Not doing anything or not following ACS protocol could negatively affect the patient.

Question 78: You confirm that no pulse is present and begin CPR. Your first shock should consist of?

c. One shock at 200 joules

Rationale: AHA guidelines recommend that because of such differences in waveform configuration, providers should use the manufacturer’s recommended energy dose (120 to 200 J) for its respective waveform. A starting energy dose of 50 J would not be considered adequate for defibrillation and is more in line with a cardioversion dose. Three stacked shocks are no longer recommended by the AHA.

Question 79: You are called to a youth summer camp for a 12 year old girl having difficulty breathing. En route to the camp you are told that a group of kids were having lunch when a hive of bees was disturbed near by. The kids took off running and when they stopped the patient began having a hard time breathing. She has no known allergies. What is the best course of action?

b. Ask the girl if she is choking. Initiate treatment and immediate transport in a position of comfort.

Rationale: Before you initiate any treatment for this patient you will want to confirm the cause of the breathing difficulty if you can. Just because there are bees present do not assume that she is going into anaphalaxis. The kids were having lunch and there is a good chance that the girl has an airway obstruction caused by food. Do not put an oxygen mask on a patient who has a possible FBAO as it may excacerbate the respiratory problems.

Question 80: The duration of the QRS in V1 and/or V2 must be how many seconds to diagnose a right or left bundle branch block?

b. 0.12 seconds or greater

Rationale: One criteria for identifying a bundle branch block using a 12 lead is the QRS in leads V1 and/or V2 must be 0.12 seconds (3 small boxes) or greater. This is an indicator of a bundle branch block.

Question 81: Your patient is a 3 year old girl who has attempted to ingest a penny. She is pale and has nasal flaring and intercostal retractions during inhalation that is accompanied by stridor. Her pulse is 70 and her movements are sluggish. With regard to respiratory arrest, which of the above signs is the most ominous?

b. Her pulse is 70

Rationale: Bradycardia is the worst sign. Anything under 80 beats per minute for a child and 100 beats per minute for an infant should be considered life threatening. If an infant or child has a pulse of less than 60 beats per minute AND they have poor systematic perfusion, CPR should be initiated.

Question 82: You are ordered by Medical Control to intubate a patient. What is the most important thing that needs to be done while you are preparing your equipment?

b. Have your assistant pre-oxygenate the patient

Rationale: Although all of the answers are things that should be done, the best choice of answer and most important is that your patient is receiving an adequate supply of oxygen and proper ventilations.

Question 83: Which of the answers correctly describe this 12-lead?

a. This patient is in rapid A-fib and is currently taking cardiac medication.

Rationale: The first thing to notice when analyzing this 12-lead is the rhythm is irregularly irregular, which indicates A-fib. The rate is approx 150bpm, which makes this rapid A-fib. Look at leads v5 and v6 you will see a dip with the S wave. This is often called a digitalis dip, from taking digoxin which is a powerful cardiac medication prescribed for a variety of reasons including A-fib. Answer B- rhythm is not sinus and there is barely, if any depression in II, III, and aVF; It needs to be at least .5mm or more to be considered ischemia. Answer C- if the rhythm was sinus it would be considered SVT (over 150) but as explained above v4, v5, and v6 do not have ST depression but rather digitalis dip. Answer D- the patient is in rapid A-fib and right ventricular hypertrophy can be seen by a large upright R wave in v1 that slowly decreases through v2, v3, and v4.

Question 84: Your cardiac arrest patient has a return of spontaneous circulation. The patient's blood pressure has dropped below 90 systolic and medical direction has ordered an Epinephrine infusion. What is the correct formula?

c. .1-.5 mcg/kg per minute

Rationale: 2010 ACLS guidelines state, "If the patient's BP is below 90 after ROSC, a Vasopressor infusion of Dopamine, Epinephrine, or Norepinephrine would be in order based on protocol." An epinenphrine infusion is .1-.5 mcg/kg per minute. For example: If you had a 50kg patient, the infusion rate would be between 5-25mcg per minute. It is important to know any drug calculation from the ACLS guidelines. Questions such as these could be asked on your NREMT exam, so know your formulas.

Question 85: It's 7:30 a.m. and you arrive on scene of a two car collision involving at least 6 patients on a foggy corner of a fairly busy country road. The fire department is not there yet and there is smoke and flames showing from both cars. You can hear people crying and cars are already driving around the wreckage to get past the scene. What steps should you take?

b. Get the fire department en route, establish a safety zone and assist in keeping traffic a safe distance away

Rationale: Scene safety before all else in this case. The best thing you can do for everybody is assist in keeping the accident from getting even larger with traffic and crowd control until the proper authorities get there and you can administer medical attention in a safe environment.

Question 86: You and your partner Bob are just pulling up to a call for a man down with CPR in progress. Dispatch has told you that the man has an extensive cardiac history and had just finished golfing with friends when he collapsed in the parking lot. According to the AHA which of the sequences is most correct?

c. BSI, Check pulse, Begin compressions, Open airway

Rationale: 2010 guidelines use CAB- Chest Compressions, Airway, and Breathing. 2005 guidelines used ABC. This is the biggest change in the new guidelines. 2010 guidelines recommend to immediately begin compressions rather than opening the patient's airway and beginning ventilations as in the 2005 guidelines. Rescuers should recognize agonal gasps/ineffective breathing, and unresponsiveness as signs of cardiac arrest, but begin CPR with compressions. An AED should be used as soon as possible when the rescuer has witnessed the arrest.

Question 87: You arrive on scene to find a 50 year old male unconscious for unknown reasons. His pulse is weak and he is breathing at approximately 20 shallow breaths per minute. A blood glucose reading shows 360 mg/dL. Which of the following answer choices contains the most correct treatment?

a. Have your partner take manual c-spine stabilization, apply O2 at 10 LPM via NRB and give a 20mL/kg bolus of normal saline.

Rationale: While assisting ventilations could become necessary the patient is currently within accepted respiratory range. The dosage for glucagon is .5 to 1.0 ml not 2.0. Insulin is rarely administered in the field and would NEVER be done without consulting medical control. Oral glucose is NOT given via IV.

Question 88: You and your partner Duval arrive on scene to find a woman who has suffered a blunt trauma to the chest from a swing on a carnival ride. She is having difficulty breathing and upon auscultation you hear nothing on the right side. This woman likely has a_____ and would be suffering from_____as the collapsed lung is incapable of oxygenating any blood.

b. Pneumothorax / hypoxia

Rationale: No breath sounds on one side is characteristic of a pneumothorax or collapsed lung. This condition would make oxygenation of the blood difficult at half capacity and cause the patient to be hypoxic.

Question 89: During an assessment, a person was found to have wet lung sounds. In what position should they be transported?

a. Semi Fowler's

Rationale: Keeping the head and chest elevated will allow for better respiratory function in the patient with wet lung sounds. It will prevent pooling of the fluids in the lungs.

Question 90: A child between 3-5 would have normal vitals if they were?

d. 20 breaths a minute, pulse of 100, and Systolic BP of 110

Rationale: A child between 3 and 5 (preschool-age) should have respirations between 20-30, a pulse of 80-120, and a systolic BP of 80 - 110.

Question 91: Your patient is a 69 year male who only responds to painful stimuli by opening his eyes briefly. Your partner initiates airway management and starts an IV while you connect the monitor. The monitor shows this rhythm. What would be the next appropriate treatment?

b. Initiate trans cutaneous pacing

Rationale: The EKG reading is a second-degree type II heart block (Mobitz) and the appropriate treatment would be to initiate trans cutaneous pacing. You will also want to consider sedating the patient with an appropriate sedative per your protocol. In the prehospital setting drug therapy is not indicated to treat a Second degree Type II heart block.

Question 92: You arrive on scene to a 71 year old female with acute onset chest pain. She's pale, dyspneic, diaphoretic and denies cardiac history. Your partner applies oxygen while you attach a 4-lead with no obvious findings. Your 12-lead shows 1mm ST elevation in leads v3 and v4. What type of infarction is this patient having?

c. Anterior

Rationale: 1mm ST elevation in two contiguous leads defines an infarction. Leads v3 and v4 look at the anterior portion of the heart.   If the patient is having ST elevation in leads v1 and v2 the patient is having a Septal Infarction. If the Patient is having ST elevation in leads v5 and v6 the patient would be having a Lateral infarction. Remember v1 and v2 are placed over the top middle of the heart that looks down through the septal part of the heart. v3 and v4 are placed over the left anterior part of the heart and v5 and v6 are placed left lateral part of the heart.

Question 93: Which of the following statements regarding helicopter safety is most accurate?

c. Rotor blades may dip as low as 4 feet off the ground

Rationale: The most accurate statement regarding helicopter safety is that their rotors can dip very low to the ground. You should be aware of this when approaching the aircraft.

Question 94: You arrive on scene where a 63 year old male is complaining of tenderness in the lower left side of his abdomen, fever, chills, and loss of appetite. After speaking with him you discover he has also had irregular bowel habits. Which of the following conditions causes such symptoms?

a. Diverticulitis

Rationale: Diverticulitis occurs when the diverticula become obstructed with fecal matter. These obstructions result in symtpoms such as irregular bowel habits (combined diarrhea and constipation), fever, and lower left quadrant pain. Half of people over 60 will experience this condition. Pancreatitis is an inflamation of the pancreas and results in such symptoms as nausea, vomitinng, tenderness, and distention of the abdomen. Cholecystitis is an inflammation of the gallbladder that results in such symptoms as the sudden onset of pain that radiates in the right upper quadrant, vomit that is described as bitter, and bile stained vomit. Acute Hepatitis is when the liver is inflamed and results in weakness, anorexia, intermittent nausea and vomitting, and pain in the right upper quadrant.

Question 95: You arrive on scene to find a 25-year-old woman with a red swollen eye who is complaining of pain and a burning sensation. After interview, you determine the patient accidentally splashed oven cleaner in her eye and is suffering a chemical burn to the eye. What is the best treatment for this patient?

c. Insertion of a Morgan Lens

Rationale: A Morgan Lens is a concave sterile plastic device which fits over the ocular globe and allows copious irrigation of the eye. It has tubing that allows it to be connected to an irrigation source. Oven cleaner has a high pH and alkaline burns are not self-limiting. They will continue to burn tissue deeper and deeper until the substance is removed or flushed from the skin. The best treatment for the patient is copious irrigation of the eye using a Morgan Lens.

Question 96: You are responding to a house fire where the report comes in that there is only one patient. He has burns that cover both of his legs. He is conscious and breathing. There are no other injuries reported. What percentage of his body is burned according to the rule of nines?

d. 36 Percent

Rationale: Each leg of an adult constitutes 18% of the body surface.

Question 97: A person who is wet _____.

b. Should not be defibrillated

Rationale: Do not shock a person who is wet.

Question 98: You arrive on scene to find a 78 year old man who is sitting in a chair and staring off into space. His breathing is labored and you can hear wet lung sounds. You get no response when you try to get his name. Your requests for him to move his toes go without response. He winces and withdraws slightly when his chest is rubbed. What is this patients GCS?

a. 9

Rationale: No verbal response gets him a 1, withdrawal from pain gets him 4 points, and his eyes being open on their own gets him 4, for a total of 9.

Question 99: Incident Command has made you transportation officer at a multiple casualty incident. A walking bridge at a nearby park has collapsed and there were 10-20 people on the bridge suffering varying degrees of injuries. You have two hospitals at your disposal. Santa Cruz Hospital is 3 miles away and Valley Hospital is 15 miles away. Which of the following transportation choices would be the BEST?

a. Send all the red tagged patients to Santa Cruz until they are at capacity. Then send any remaining red tagged patients to Valley Hospital followed by yellow and green tagged patients.

Rationale: Among all the choices, the most appropriate would be to send the priority one (red) patients to the nearest hospital, and the less priority patients (yellow and green) to the hospital further away. This can be altered based on the need of a specialized treatment center. For example: If you have a yellow tagged pediatric patient, and the closest hospital is the pediatric center.

Question 100: A call comes in for a 61 yr old female with an altered LOC. When you arrive, the patient's sister tells you that the patient had a stroke about a year ago, but she knows of no other health problems. During your initial assessment, you find her eyes open and looking around. She is speaking to you, but saying inappropriate words. She will not obey your commands to "raise your arm please ma'am" and she moves her arm toward her chest when you give her a light sternal rub. What is this woman's GCS and what should you do after administering oxygen?

a. GCS of 12 / Package the patient for transport

Rationale: The woman's eyes are open spontaneously so she gets a 4. She is speaking inappropriate words and this gets her a 3. You know she will not obey commands, but will localize pain which gets her a 5, which nets her a GCS of 12. Given the history and the altered LOC, immediate transport is the next best thing to do.

Question 101: You are dispatched to a boat fire with multiple victims in the water. You are the only Paramedic on scene. Upon arrival you find patient #1 shivering uncontrollably, but able to answer questions appropriately. Patient #2 is on a boat across the bay with another EMS unit. That unit relates that the patient is mildly hypothermic and doesn't want to be transported. Both patients indicate that a third person was with them and that he was burned badly. On scene command confirms that this patient is still in the water. Which is the most critical patient, and why?

c. Patient #3, because he will require the most care when he is removed from the water.

Copyright 2013 EMT-National-Training

Rationale: Patient #3 is triaged as the most critical, even though you haven't seen him. Patient #1 is in mild hypothermia, and can be treated at the BLS level with warming measures. Patient #2 has been assessed and is refusing transport, so he is not your concern. There is no such thing as hypogenic shock.

Question 102: The Intrasseous route (IO) is in which category of drug administration?

c. Parenteral Route

Rationale: The Intraosseous route (IO) is in the parenteral route category which is drugs administered by injection. The IO route is injected directly into the bone marrow cavity. Others include subcutaneous, intramuscular, intravenous, intradermal, and endotracheal. Enteral route includes Oral, gastric, and rectal. An example of dermal is nitropaste where it absorbs through the skin.

Question 103: You and your partner Loni arrive on scene to find 4 patients. Which one of them would be your priority?

c. A 7 year old who is conscious, with respirations of 27, and a systolic of 68 mm Hg

Rationale: The key to this answer is knowing that a child with a blood pressure lower than 70 mm Hg is considered critical. A patient this age should have a systolic around 100.

Question 104: What would you do if a newborn infant has a heart rate lower than 100 beats a minute?

a. Ventilate at 40-60 breaths a minute

Rationale: You should ventilate at 40 to 60 breaths a minute. If the infant is below 60 beats a minute, you should do chest compressions as well for a total of 120 events per minute(90 compressions and 30 breaths).

Question 105: You and your AEMT partner are dispatched to a 34 year old male with chest pain. As you approach the patient you notice he is breathing fast and holding his chest. He is able to talk to you in complete sentences and does not appear to have a diminished LOC. He states he has been under a lot of emotional stress with work and just found out his girlfriend is pregnant. He also tells you he does not have a cardiac history and feels light headed. Your partner obtains a set of vital signs while you attach a cardiac monitor. Your partner relates that the patient is breathing at 27 breaths per minute, has a blood pressure of 98/62, and a rapid pulse. Once you have the monitor attached you observe sinus tach at 175 beats a minute with a narrow QRS. After attaching oxygen and having your partner start an IV what would be the next appropriate intervention?

a. Ask the patient "to bear down" in an attempt to slow the heart rate

Rationale: 2010 ACLS guidelines states that for a patient in SVT that is not hypotensive, does not have an altered LOC, and has a narrow QRS (basically does not appear symptomatic), the first intervention after oxygen and IV is to use vagal maneuvers. If this is not effective than Adenosine would be the next appropriate treatment. You would only want to use synchronized cardioversion if the patient was hypotensive, had an altered LOC and was presenting symptomatic. Make sure to have your ACLS algorithms memorized.

Question 106: You arrive on scene of a 49 year old female with shortness of breath. The patients' family reports to you that she has a long standing history of COPD. You note that the patient appears to have labored breathing with audible expiratory wheezes with a respiratory rate of 36. The patient is only able to speak in 1-2 word sentences and has ashen skin color. You instruct your partner to being ventilation of this patient with a BVM. Your next course of action for this patient should be?

b. Place a PEEP valve on the BVM and ventilate the patient.

Rationale: The best treatment for this patient would be to continue BVM ventilation and attaching a PEEP valve. By using a PEEP valve, you are maximizing the ventilatory effort of your patient by assisting with the prevention of alveolar collapse that is occurring. Due to the lack of surfactant within the alveoli, they begin to stick "shut". Although a nebulizer treatment would also be indicated for this patient, their respiratory rate is rapid and needs to be assisted so that the medications will be inhaled completely to work.

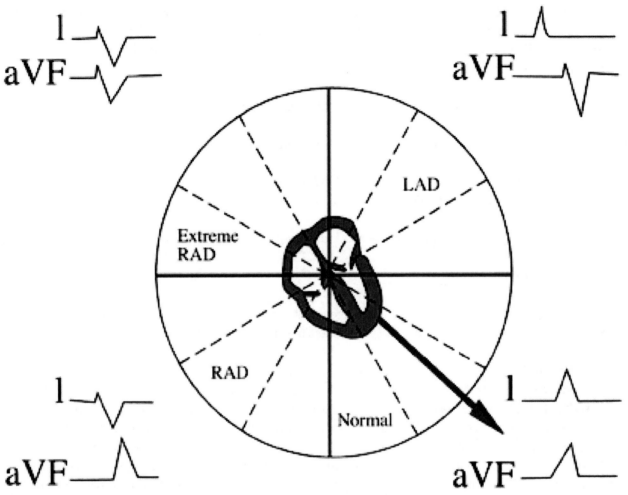

Question 107: If a patient has an upright QRS in Lead I and an upright QRS in Lead AVF, how would you describe their Axis Deviation

c. Normal Axis Deviation

Rationale: If both QRS's in leads I and AVF are positive, that means they have Normal Axis Deviation. The hearts conduction system is starting in the right atrium and ending in the left ventricle.

Question 108: Cardiogenic shock could be brought on by:

a. A heart attack

Rationale: Cardio, referring to the heart, would indicate that a heart attack is responsible. A state of shock brought on by fright would be psychogenic.

Question 109: Which of the following statements is true with regard to American Heart Association Advanced Cardiovascular Life Support (ACLS)?

d. Effective ACLS begins with high quality BLS and CPR

Rationale: Major changes in ACLS now make IV or IO the preferred route of drug administration. Drugs should be delivered AFTER rhythm check, not before. Providers should not check for rhythm or pulse after shock. Do 5 cycles of CPR and then check.

Question 110: The right side of the heart _____ and _____.

b. receives systemic circulation, drives pulmonary circulation

Rationale: The right side of the heart receives systemic circulation and drives pulmonary circulation.

Question 111: You and your partner Scott are called to a trailer court for a behavioral problem. When you arrive, law enforcement is already on scene and have a man in his mid 20's handcuffed. The man is very thin and does not have a shirt on. His hair is all messed up and there is a gash on his shoulder that is still bleeding. As your partner begins treating the wound, the arresting officer tells you that a neighbor called law enforcement when the man was seen eating out of a cat food dish on the neighbor's porch. Your initial assessment shows the man has an altered LOC and will not answer any questions or make eye contact. His respiration rate appears to be normal with adequate volume and his pulse is strong and rapid at 120. His skin is pale looking and cool to the touch. What is most likely wrong with this man? How would you treat him?

b. He is hypoglycemic. Get a blood glucose reading from a fresh finger stick. Bandage the wound and administer one tube of glucose if the blood sugar reading is low.

Rationale: The altered level of consciousness, extreme hunger, rapid pulse, and pale skin should lead you to believe that this man's main problem is depleted glucose levels. He may have a mental health issue, but treating him and then turning him over to law enforcement may constitute abandonment. He could also be on narcotics, but transporting him strapped down would be unnecessary at this point. Applying an antiseptic to the wound should be left to the hospital staff.

Question 112: According to 2010 ACLS guidelines, what is the most important intervention an ACLS provider can do to improve a defibrillation attempt?

b. Chest compressions

Rationale: ACLS guidelines state good quality chest compressions are the most important thing you can do in aiding a successful defibrillation. For this reason, AHA has changed to C.A.B from the old ABC. Remember that if you do the basics really well to begin with, it will improve the outcome of the advanced skills if you have to use them.

Question 113: Which of the following is not a way that CPAP can be applied?

d. Through a levin tube

Rationale: CPAP can be applied through a face mask, nose mask, and invasively through an ET Tube. A Levin Tube is a type of nasogastric tube, and CPAP cannot be applied through a nasogastric tube.

Question 114: A fierce winter storm has left hundreds of people stranded along a stretch of highway for a few days. You have been dispatched with the National Guard to help care for anyone suffering from exposure. As you prepare your equipment what things should you carry extra of and why?

b. Drinking water; Dehydration is a very likely problem

Rationale: While warming methods and glucose are good, drinking water is probably the most important. This is due to the fact that cold weather decreases our thirst mechanism and so we don't drink. However, a lot of moisture is lost during the respiratory cycle in cold air. This is compounded by not feeling thirsty, and a person becomes dehydrated very quickly and doesn't realize it. It is important to encouraging patients of exposure to take fluids either hot or cold.

Question 115: Which drug and dose would be appropriate to treat rapid atrial fibrillation?

d. Cardizem .25mg/kg

Rationale: Diltiazem is the same drug as Cardizem and the correct dose is .25mg/kg. A second dose can be given at .35 mg/kg. This is usually the first drug of choice when treating a person with A-fib.

Question 116: You are assessing a 2-month-old girl who is sleeping in her crib. Which of the following signs would cause you to be concerned?

c. Difficulty waking the child up / persistent crying

Rationale: An infant who will not easily wake should be considered an emergency. Babies sleep a lot, but should wake up easily when roused. Persistent crying in young infants can also be a sign of significant illness. Children often cry or whimper when waking up. This is not generally associated with illness or trauma. Children this age have very limited head control and it is not unusual for a 2 month old to lack the ability to hold up it's head. Drooling and fluttering eyelashes while sleeping are common and not normally something to be concerned with.

Question 117: You are treating a patient who is complaining of chest pain. They are diaphoretic with a blood pressure of 98/50. You have their medications on board which include a prescription for nitroglycerin. Medical control has instructed you to administer 1 nitroglycerin tablet sublingually. How would you respond?

d. Repeat the vital signs to medical control and ask if they still wish to have you administer the nitroglycerin with the blood pressure that low.

Rationale: Administering nitroglycerin is contraindicated in patients with a blood pressure of less than 100 (Systolic), however it is always the best option to repeat the information to medical control if they give an order you think might be dangerous. Many doctors would have no problem with administering nitroglycerin to a patient who has a borderline BP, but you want to make sure they understand your concern. Ultimately you are an extension of the medical direction and unless you are sure the prescribed treatment will cause harm, you should follow the directions after clarifying the information. You should never blindly follow orders however. You need to make informed and educated treatment decisions.

Question 118: You arrive on scene to find a 34 year old male laying on the ground in a pool of blood. Bright red blood is spurting from a large cut in his shirt sleeve and he is clutching a knife between his teeth. What should you do first?

d. Leave the scene until police arrive to make the scene safe

Rationale: Scene safety comes before all other choices and until the police arrive AND secure the scene you are to keep a safe distance and advise others to do the same. You are not in a position to render this scene safe.

Question 119: The immune system can over react to normally harmless foreign material. This normally harmless material is called a/n _____.

a. Antigen

Rationale: An antigen is a foreign particle or substance that is not normally dangerous, but the body treats it as if it were.

Question 120: What description below best describes Portal Hypertension?

c. Portal Hypertension is due to liver disease commonly found in alcoholics, which can lead to a variety of disorders including ascites and esophogeal varices.

Rationale: Portal Hypertension is caused by liver damage commonly found in Alcoholics. Increased resistance to flow through the systemic venous system and the portal system forces blood through alternate channels. The increased demand on the alternate vessels causes varices and ascites. There are medications that affect blood pressure but they are simply called medication-induced hypertension. Some pregnant woman, not necessarily obese, can become hypertensive, which is called pre-eclampsia. The last answer is the correct definition of Malignant Hypertension but it's not known as Portal Hypertension.

Question 121: Identify this rhythm, and which intervention would be appropriate based on the patients signs and symptoms. Patient is a 62 year old female who has been having episodes of syncope. When you arrive on scene she is not responsive when you talk to her, and moans when you give her a sternal rub. She has a history of hypertension and is currently on Propranolol. She appears to be in respiratory distress. Her BP is 88/52, and her pulse is slow and weak.

b. Third Degree; Give oxygen via NRB 15L, start an IV, and immediately begin transcutaneous pacing.

Rationale: The rhythm is a Third Degree heart block. Note the disassociation between atrial and ventricular complexes. The patient is symptomatic based on her ALOC, hypotension and dyspnea. The appropriate treatment is to begin oxygen therapy, IV, and start pacing. Also consider sedation and pain management while pacing.

Question 122: What is the name of the protein that binds oxygen to the red blood cell?

c. Hemoglobin

Rationale: Hemoglobin binds oxygen to the red blood cell. Erythrocytes is another name for red blood cells or RBCs. Another name for white blood cells is leukocytes. Plasma is the fluid or water portion of the blood.

Question 123: After recognition of asystole on your cardiac monitor, you should do what?

a. Confirm in a second lead

Rationale: Fine V-Fib may be masked in one lead but not another so it is advised to confirm asystole in a second lead.

Question 124: You arrive on scene to find a man in his 70's lying on his bed experiencing extreme abdominal pain. He said he has a long history of cirrhosis and alcoholism. As you are doing your physical exam you expose his abdomen to find it severely distended. What is this commonly called, and how would you treat this patient?

a. Ascites- airway management, IV, 100mcg of fentanyl, and transport in position of comfort

Rationale: Ascites is a build up of fluid in the peritoneal cavity. The patient is usually thin with a massive abdomen. It is commonly caused by liver damage due to alcoholism. The only treatment recommended is airway and pain management.

Question 125: BSI is a concept that considers all body tissue and body fluids as having the potential for being infectious. Who is responsible for creating this universal set of guidelines?

d. All of the above

Rationale: Along with several other agencies including the NFPA and OSHA, these guidelines were developed as safety precautions for the workplace.

Question 126: A woman has just given birth to a healthy baby boy with the assistance of her partner. The delivery went fine, but during the delivery of the placenta she began to hemorrhage. The best course of treatment would include?

b. Massage the uterus, treat for shock, and transport

Rationale: Massaging the uterus may help to stop the bleeding. Rapid transport to the ER and O2 are advised because of the potential shock danger with the loss of blood in quantity.

Question 127: If a patient, whom you believe is of sound mind, denies medical attention even though you know it would be in their best interest to be treated, the best thing you could do is?

a. Try to convince them again and be honest about what their condition is and the possible risks of refusal.

Rationale: Being truthful and honest with regard to how the refusal of medical care may prove to be dangerous and life threatening is the best approach. If you cannot convince the patient and you believe they are of sound mind your best option is to have them sign a refusal form and leave.

Question 128: Describe what is happening in this waveform.

b. Patient is hypoventilating

Rationale: The best answer is the patient is hypoventilating. You can see this by waveform slowly rising. The patient is not breathing adequately enough, so the CO2 continues to buildup in the patient's lungs, causing the taller waveform.

Question 129: The National Incident Management System (NIMS) includes a componant referred to as "Interoperability". This componant is concerned with:

c. Communication between EMS, fire and law enforcement during an MCI.

Rationale: Interoperability is an important issue for law enforcement, fire fighting, EMS, and other public health and safety departments, because first responders need to be able to communicate during wide-scale emergencies.

Question 130: You and your partner Ashley arrive at a house where dispatch reports a 911 call was made. Nobody was on the phone to report any emergency, and attempts at calling back have resulted in a busy signal. A frantic woman exits the house screaming about her daughter not breathing. You enter the home to find a 9 year old girl lying supine on the kitchen floor very cyanotic. After 2 rescue breaths, each given over a period of _____, you begin ventilations with a BVM at a rate of _____ and a tidal volume of _____.

d. 1 second / 12-20 breaths per minute / enough air to cause adequate chest rise

Rationale: AHA guidelines have rescue breaths performed over 1 second. Proper ventilation rates for children are now 12-20 breaths per minute. Tidal volume is no longer referred to in ml. The volume of each breath should be "just enough to cause adequate chest rise."

Question 131: Without any further information, what condition would you say the following patient is in? A 1-year-old male with a pulse rate of 110, breathing at 30 breaths per minute, with a systolic BP of 90.

a. Good

Rationale: All vitals are within normal limits for a child of this age. 1-year-old is the dividing line between infancy and toddler age, and so both sets of vital sign ranges could apply to a 1-year-old. Treat the patient based on overall appearance and what the parents tell you is normal or abnormal.

Question 132: Using lights and sirens during a cardiac arrest transport is?

c. A consideration for moving quickly and safely through traffic

Rationale: Using lights and sirens should have a purpose. Sometimes it is the last thing in the world you want. Using lights and sirens to safely and quickly expedite a patient is acceptable and expected.

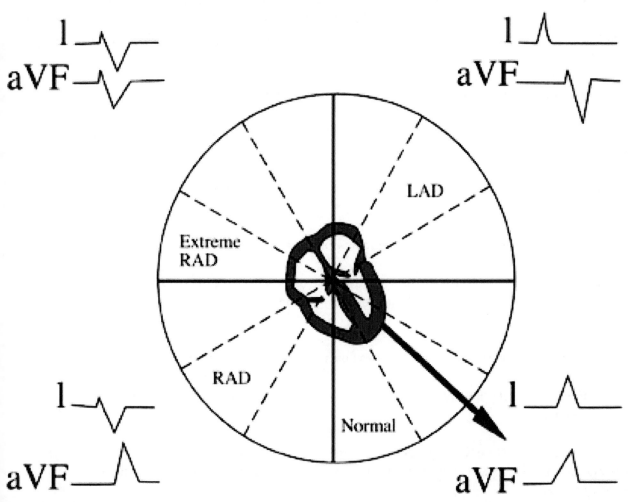

Question 133: If a patient has a negative QRS in Lead I and a negative QRS in Lead AVF, how would you describe their Axis Deviation?

d. Extreme Right Axis Deviation

Rationale: If both QRS's in leads I and AVF are negative, that means they have Extreme Right Axis Deviation. A way to remember is to imagine leads I and AVF are your thumbs, if the QRS in both leads is positive, thumbs up, it is Normal Axis Deviation. If the QRS in both leads is negative, thumbs down, that indicates Extreme Right Axis Deviation and serious depolarization issues.

Question 134: After treating a patient in cardiac arrest you find a Return of Spontaneous Circulation, the patient's Blood Pressure has dropped below 85 systolic and medical direction has ordered Norepinephrine Infusion. What is the correct formula?

a. .1-.5 mcg/kg per minute

Rationale: 2010 ACLS guidelines state, "If the patients BP is below 90 after ROSC, a Vasopressor infusion of Dopamine, Epinephrine, or Norepinephrine would be in order based on protocol." A Norepinenphrine infusion is .1-.5 mcg/kg per minute. For example: If you had a 90kg patient the infusion rate would be between 9-45mcg per minute. It is important to know any drug calculation from the ACLS guidelines. These types of questions could be asked on your NREMT exam, so know your formulas.

Question 135: You arrive on scene with your partner Emilio to find a woman who is having problems breathing. She is speaking in 1 or 2 word bursts and is on oxygen at 3 liters per minute. There is an ashtray next to her bed loaded with cigarette butts. She says her care taker called the ambulance and she does not want you there. She says she will allow you to take her vitals but then you have to leave. Her BP is 100/60 her pulse is 48 and her respirations are 18. She says she is 89 years old and has a pacemaker and is on high blood pressure medication. "I just want to be old, please leave", she says. What should you do?

c. Respect her wishes and leave, asking her to please call if she needs medical attention

Rationale: As long as the patient is of sound mind you must respect their request to be left alone. Reminding her that you are a phone call away is not a bad idea.

Question 136: While trying to determine why your patient is in cardiac arrest, which of the following is a correct list of reversible causes?

a. Hypoxia, Hydrogen Ion, Hypokalemia, Toxins, Thrombosis-pulmonary

Rationale: According to the 2010 ACLS guidelines the list of reversible causes are as follows: Hypovolemia, Hypoxia, Hydrogen ion (acidosis) Hypo/Hyperkalemia, Hypothermia, Tension Pneumothorax, Tamponade-Cardiac, Toxins, Thrombosis-coronary, and Thrombosis-pulmonary.

Question 137: Continuous positive airway pressure (CPAP) is best described by which of the following definitions?

b. Positive pressure transmitted into the airways of a patient allowing for better diffusion of gases and re-expansion of collapsed alveoli.

Rationale: B is the correct answer. CPAP is continuous positive airway pressure, splinting the airways and alveoli open to facilitate gas exchange. A is the description of orogastric intubation. C describes Endotracheal intubation. D describes positive end expiratory pressure.

Question 138: The process of glucose being broken down within the cell is called?

a. Biochemical process

Rationale: The process of glucose being broken down is bio - body chemical.

Question 139: How would you appropriately treat a patient with a pulmonary embolism?

a. Continued oxygen, administer lactated ringer solution, rapid transport in a position of comfort.

Rationale: A patient with a pulmonary embolism is a true emergency; unfortunately as a paramedic we are unable to definitively treat this patient. Our treatment is limited to providing oxygen therapy, administering fluid such as normal saline and lactated ringer's, and rapid transport in a position of comfort. Definitive care for this patient requires fibrinolytic or heparin therapy.

Question 140: While performing CPR on a 72 year old patient, you attempt to identify any reversible causes. Which of the following is a correct list of reversible causes?

d. Toxins, Tamponade-cardiac, Thrombosis-coronary, Hypovolemia, Hypokalemia

Rationale: According to the 2010 ACLS guidelines the list of reversible causes are as follows: Hypovolemia, Hypoxia, Hydrogen ion (acidosis) Hypo/Hyperkalemia, Hypothermia, Tension Pneumothorax, Tamponade-Cardiac, Toxins, Thrombosis-coronary, Thrombosis-pulmonary

Question 141: Which of the following are the correct dose and route for oral glucose?

c. 15g buccal

Rationale: The correct dose and route for oral glucose is 15g. Oral glucose comes in a tube containing a gel with 15 grams of dextrose. The proper route of administration is buccal, or between the teeth and gums.

Question 142: You arrive on scene with your partner Joe to find an 7 year old boy unconscious after being dragged from the water. He is not breathing and has no pulse. CPR in this case should include_____.

b. 15:2 compression to ventilation ratio

Rationale: AHA CPR Guidelines specify that for two person CPR on a child you should use a 15:2 ratio. It would be 30:2 if you were alone and did not have your partner Joe.

Question 143: You are assisting your partner who is preparing to intubate a 79 year old woman. You are managing the BVM and begin ventilating and preoxygenating the patient at what rate?

c. 12-20 breaths a minute for 1-2 minutes

Rationale: Pre oxygenating and hyperventilating a patient prior to intubation should be done at a rate of 12-20 breaths per minute for 1-2 minutes with high flow O2 attached.

Question 144: All of the following are considered stimulants except:

a. Chloroquine

Rationale: Stimulants produce an excited state and include: Amphetamine, methamphetamine, phentermine hydrochloride, ecstasy, eve, cocaine, PCP, and methaqualone.

Question 145: You and your partner arrive at the home of a 59 year old male with a history of acute pulmonary edema. The patient is conscious and breathing at a rate of 28 breaths/min. Which treatment is best indicated?

d. use a Continous Positive Airway Pressure (CPAP) device.

Rationale: Research is showing that CPAP has better results with fewer problems than the more traditional methods used in the past. While this device may not be in use in many parts of the country yet, it is now included in the National EMS Education Standards as a recommended treatment at the EMT level.

Question 146: A patient with heat exhaustion who is fully alert should be encouraged to?

d. Sit up and slowly drink a liter of water as long as they don't feel nauseated

Rationale: If they are alert and oriented the best thing the patient can do is drink some water and they need to be moved to a location that is much cooler. Be prepared for a patient to become nauseated.

Question 147: You are first on scene to an MVA involving two cars. The crash scene is only blocking the south bound lane of traffic and cars from both directions are taking turns using the open north bound lane to pass the crash scene. What is your first priority?

c. To ensure traffic is controlled properly and the scene is safe

Rationale: Scene safety is your first priority. The cars driving past present a very real threat to everyone working on the scene, as well as the patients.

Question 148: Which of the following statements best describes Axis Deviation?

b. Refers to the direction of depolorization through the heart.

Rationale: Axis deviation refers to the direction of depolarization through the heart. Normal Axis deviation would start in the right atrium and end in the left ventricle because the left ventricle is typically stronger than the right ventricle. This means if a patient had infarcted tissue from an MI in the left ventricle, more than likely the right ventricle would be working harder and the patient would have Right Axis Deviation, not Left. The best Leads to identify Axis Deviation are Leads I and AVF. 0 to -90 degrees describes Left Axis Deviation. -90 to -180 degrees describes Extreme Right Axis Deviation.

Question 149: You are on your way back from lunch when you come upon a two vehicle collision that is blocking an intersection. Both cars are engulfed in flames. What would be the best choice of action?

b. Keep your distance until the danger is under control

Rationale: The best choice of answer is to keep your distance until the danger is under control. Entering the collision area would be entering an unsafe scene. Calling for Hazmat and getting the ambulance extinguisher may be things you would do, but they are NOT the best choice of action.

Question 150: Which answer below best defines a right bundle branch block?

a. Right bundle branch is blocked and the electric impulses must find an alternate pathway to depolarize the right side of the heart

Rationale: Answer A best describes a right bundle branch block. From the Bundle of His the conduction pathway splits into right and left branches that allow electric impulses to travel down each branch and depolarize both the right and left ventricle simultaneously. With an RBBB the right bundle branch has a block and the electrical impulse must find an alternate pathway to the right ventricle. This causes a delay and the ventricles do not depolarize simultaneously. Answer B describes LBBB, Answer C describes right-sided heart failure, and Answer D describes an infarct.

Question 151: When treating a patient suffering from hypothermia what should you avoid doing?

a. Focused, active warming of the extremities to raise the body temperature.

Rationale: Rough handling of a hypothermic patient can result in an increased risk of life threatening dysrhythmias including VF and asystole. Active rewarming of the extremities alone can cause reflex vasodilation and lead to shock. Heat packs used for warming may cause burns if placed directly on the skin and may not be used if transport times are of a short duration.

Question 152: Continuing with above scenario. You begin pacing and obtain electrical and mechanical capture. You reassess his vitals, blood pressure is now 96/50, respirations are 13 breaths per minute with 96% oxygen saturation. There are 2 hospitals nearby; the first hospital is 5 minutes away with a fully staffed ER. The second hospital is 20 minutes away with a fully staffed ER and cath lab. Based on your patients current condition which is the preferred hospital and what is your report?

d. It is important to transport him to the hospital 20 minutes away with the cath lab. Your report should include signs and symptoms, 12 lead findings, interventions done, and ETA.

Rationale: D is your best choice. The only thing that will ultimately save this patient's life is a cath lab. The patient is deteriorating because his heart is infarcting. Taking him to the closest hospital would only be wasting time. During your report you need to include patient's signs and symptoms, interventions done, 12 lead findings, and ETA to the receiving hospital. The hospital can in turn be prepared to take the patient to the cath lab as soon as you arrive.

Question 153: AHA Guidelines specify that rescue breaths should be delivered over a period of_____.

a. 1 second

Rationale: According to AHA CPR Guidelines rescue breaths should be delivered over 1 second.

Question 154: The apothecary system is for _____.

b. Measuring dosage of medications

Rationale: It is the system of measuring medication.

Question 155: What would you do if a new born infant does not begin spontaneously breathing after suctioning?

b. Vigorous but gentle rubbing of the infants back

Rationale: First give the infant a vigorous back rub with light pressure to stimulate breathing. If that does not work you should begin ventilating.

Question 156: You are a paramedic treating a patient in respiratory arrest. You were able to secure an ET tube after your third attempt. Your partner notices the patient's stomach is extremely distended from your previous attempts at ventilating esophageal intubations, he orders you to insert an NG tube. What do you do?

d. Make sure you have all the supplies you need and begin proper insertion of an NG tube.

Rationale: The most appropriate answer is to make sure you have everything you need and insert an NG tube. The ET tube does not affect proper placement of an NG tube. It is not contraindicated to insert an NG tube after placement of an ET tube. Orogastric insertion is not indicated over an NG tube. Suctioning the patient's airway would be futile in removing air and contents from the stomach.

Question 157: It is the middle of winter and you and your partner are called to the scene of a homeless man having breathing problems. You arrive to find him laying on a sidewalk on a calm, but very cold night. He is likely losing heat from?

a. Conduction

Rationale: The cold pavement is likely conducting the heat away from his body. While there could be evaporation and convection at play, both of those options are less of an impact than someone who is in contact with cold concrete.

Question 158: You are suctioning an unconscious patient who has vomited. It is proper procedure to suction the patient for approximately _____ and then _____.

a. 10-15 seconds / rinse the catheter in preparation of additional suctioning

Rationale: Suctioning should not be done for a prolonged period, but the obstruction must be removed. Additionally you should not throw the catheter away, instead rinse it in sterile water in preparation for additional suctioning.

Question 159: What position should a patient be placed in to aide with the insertion of a nasogastric tube?

b. High Fowler's

Rationale: High Fowler's position is recommended because the patient is semi upright with the patient's head at about 80-90 degrees. This prevents aspiration during the insertion of the tube. Insertion of an NG tube utilizes gravity to pass the tube through the esophagus. Supine position isn't helpful because the patient is lying flat. Prone position is face down which makes insertion more difficult. Trendelenburg position is supine with the feet elevated higher than the head, which also isn't helpful.

Question 160: Your unit is called to the scene of a motor vehicle collision at a busy intersection. A man in his 40's, driving a small truck, has hit a telephone pole head on. He was unrestrained and ejected through the windshield at approximately 50 MPH. When you arrive, he has been secured to a backboard with proper c-spine precautions. His pulse is 80 beats per minute and he is breathing regularly and deeply at 12 respirations per minute. You notice that his pulse seems to weaken during inhalation. While taking his blood pressure, you see that each time he inhales, his systolic pressure drops by 20-30 mmHg. His trachea is midline and lung sounds are equal. What is the most likely reason for these vital signs?

b. Liquid filling the pericardium increases pressure and inhibits the ventricles from filling properly, which in turn leads to low stroke volume and low pressure

Rationale: This patient is exhibiting signs of cardiac tamponade and pulsus paradoxus, making answer 2 correct. Answer 1 is incorrect because the pons regulates respiration, but is not associated with pulse. Answer 3 is eluding to a tension pneumothorax, but the assessment confirms a midline trachea and equal breath sounds. Answer 4 is incorrect as injury to the spine will not cause an interference or a variant or irregular breathing pattern that causes a drop in blood pressure upon inspiration

Question 161: You are the Incident Commander at the scene of a bus rollover. A tourist group of approximately 25 senior citizens was on the bus when it overturned on a sharp corner. Which of the following actions would be appropriate?

c. Assigning a triage officer, treatment officer, and a transportation officer

Rationale: Part of the Incident Commander's responsibilities can be to assign different officers to manage the different components of the ICS. This includes triage, treatment, and transportation of the patients. The IC would not likely be physically helping with extrication as they would then not have command of the other ICS components.

Question 162: The manner in which you must act is called?

b. Standard of care

Rationale: Standard of care requires you to act and behave a certain way toward individuals.

Question 163: You are assessing an 84 year old man. Upon auscultation of the lungs you discover crackles or rale sounds. He is complaining of chest pain and congestion. These signs and symptoms can indicate?

d. Left ventricular failure

Rationale: These are signs and symptoms of a possible failure of the left ventricle. The pump portion of the heart is unable to pump efficiently and fluid begins to back up into the lungs.

Question 164: What is the most common cause of AED failure?

c. Battery failure

Rationale: Battery failure is the most common reason for AED failure. Check batteries often and service correctly.

Question 165: A 27 year old man and his 4 year old nephew have been pulled from a river after being submerged for approximately 12 minutes. Rescue breathing for the man should include breaths at what rate? Rescue breathing for the child should include breaths at what rate?

a. 1 breath every 5-6 seconds for the man / 1 breath every 3-5 seconds for the child

Rationale: AHA CPR Guidelines specify state that adults should get 10-12 breaths per minute (one breath every 5-6 seconds). Children should get between 12-20 breaths per minute (one breath every 3-5 seconds). Old guidelines said 20 bpm for all infants and children. The new wider range is to allow the rescuer to tailor rescue breathing to the needs of the patient.

Question 166: During endotracheal intubation of a child you should always?

d. Use the Broselow tape to ensure the correct tube is selected

Rationale: While the Sellick maneuver may be indicated, the Broselow tape will allow you to select the appropriate tube.

Question 167: What is one very important thing to note prior to initiating CPAP therapy on a patient?

a. How much oxygen is in the tank

Rationale: Several factors are important to note prior to using CPAP therapy. CPAP machines use large amounts of oxygen, it's very important to verify your tank is full. Failing to have enough oxygen in a tank can lead to a rapid collapse of your patient if therapy is initiated and then stops very quickly from lack of oxygen. A tight fitting mask seal is also critical to the therapies success. Finally, CPAP can lower a patient's blood pressure; be cautious with profound hypotension. Take into account skin color, distance of transport, and a patient's ability to walk as part of your overall assessment of the scene and patient, but those are not as important when deciding to begin CPAP therapy.

Question 168: Correctly interpret the EKG below:

a. Sinus rhythm with left bundle branch block

Rationale: The correct interpretation of the EKG strip is Sinus rhythm with a left bundle branch block. In v1 and v2 the QRS is negative and wider than .12, which indicates an LBBB. (Remember the turn signal method as easy guide...if the QRS is negative it indicates an LBBB, if the QRS is upright and QRS is wider than .12 this would indicate an RBBB) The presence of an LBBB eliminates the ability to confirm a myocardial infarction in the pre-hospital setting.

Question 169: You are transporting a 32 year old pregnant woman who is in the 32nd week. She is complaining of stomach pain and is pale. How would you transport her?

a. Left lateral recumbent

Rationale: A left lateral position is recommended in order to relieve potential pressure on the inferior vena cava.

Question 170: An ice storm has caused a 10 car pile up on a nearby interstate. Incident command has instructed you to take over triage of the patients. Patient 1 is a woman who has a broken arm and a back injury with suspected spinal cord damage. Patient 2 is male and has a broken femur and is showing signs of shock. Patient 3 is an elderly woman who has a laceration on her forehead and pain in her wrist. Patient 4 is a male, breathing at 6 breaths a minute with a head injury. What color triage tag should each of these patients receive?

d. 1Yellow, 2Red, 3Green, 4Red

Rationale: The first patient with the back injury is yellow tagged, even with the suspected spinal cord injury, their transport is delayed. Patient number 2 is a red tagged because of the signs of shock, they require immediate transport. Patient number 3 has only minor injuries, therefore, she gets a green tag and is transported last. Patient number 4 is having problems breathing, so it is priority one or red tag.

Question 171: Most violent injuries to first responder's occur?

c. When a patient has a sudden behavioral change

Rationale: Contrary to popular belief, most people think crime scene. However, it usually involves drugs or alcohol or behaviorally disturbed patients or bystanders.

Question 172: Correctly interpret this 12-lead.

a. Inferior Myocardial Infarction with Anterior Ischemia

Rationale: The correct interpretation is an Inferior MI with Anterior Ischemia. If you look in leads II, III, and aVF you will see ST elevation from .5mm up to almost 4mm. Remember ST-elevation 1mm or above in 2 contiguous leads with no left bundle branch block means you need to treat the patient as if he is having an MI. You also see reciprocal changes in leads I and aVL. There is ST depression in leads v3 and v4 up to 3mm, which would indicate Anterior Ischemia. In order for a patient to have a Left Bundle Branch Block they need to have a QRS .12 or wider (3 small squares) in leads v1, v2, or v5, v6. Left Axis Deviation would have an upright QRS in lead I and a negative QRS and aVF. There is no ST elevation in any of the lateral leads (I, aVL, v5, v6) so the patient is not having a lateral infarction. A Bi-fasicular Block is both a right and left Bundle Branch Block, and as stated above, the QRS would need to be .12 or wider. Left ventricular hypertrophy is determined by adding the length of the R wave in v1 and the R wave in v5, they need to equal 35mm (7 big boxes) or greater.

Question 173: You are on scene with a patient and medical control has ordred an infusion of Intropin. What drug is this?

b. Dopamine

Rationale: Intropin is the brand name for Dopamine. Proventil is the brand name for Albuterol. Pitressin is brand name for Vasopressin. Solu Medrol is the brand name for Methylprednisolone. Intoropin is a sympathomimetic that increases contractility in the heart and also causes peripheral vasoconstriction.

Question 174: You are called to the scene of a woman who is having difficulty breathing. Upon arrival you notice several people surrounding the woman who seems to be agitated. Your scene assessment determines it to be safe and you approach the woman who is in the tripod position. Her breathing is rapid and shallow. She states her ribs hurt after being struck with a punch from her husband. You should?

b. Treat the patient if the situation appears safe and inform law enforcement of the possible assault when the time is appropriate

Rationale: If you believe the scene to be safe and begin treating the patient, it would be prudent to inform the police of the supposed attack.

Question 175: When the body does not have enough insulin to break down the available sugars, it begins to consume the _____ of the body.

b. Stored fats

Rationale: The body will consume the stored fats when there is no available glucose.

Question 176: You and your partner Nick are dispatched to the scene of a small building fire, just as backup and possible rehabilitation. As you round a corner near the scene, you see 10-12 people lying in a yard a few houses away from the fire. Some are in obvious distress and others are walking aimlessly down the street.. Which of the following choices would be the most appropriate for you and Nick to take?

d. Contact the IC and notify them of the current situation, triage and order more resources through command

Rationale: Getting additional help on the way to treat multiple patients is the best choice of action.

Question 177: Your patient is a 19 year old female who is G4/P2/A1. Her boyfriend called 911 stating that the woman is a diabetic and pregnant in her third trimester. She is complaining of a headache, abdominal pain, and blurred vision. Upon arrival at the residence, you notice the woman's feet and fingers are swollen. Her pulse is 116 and her respirations are about 16 breaths per minute. The patient's blood pressure is 145/92 and auscultation of the lungs reveals rales. How many live births has this woman had? What is most likely wrong with her and how should she be treated? Choose the best answer.

a. She has had 2 live births. She has preeclampsia and should be transported to the hospital in a left lateral position while on high flow O2. Initiate an IV line TKO if protocols and scope of practice allow.

Rationale: G stands for Gravida or "pregnancies", P stands for Para or "live births" and A stands for "abortion", elective or spontaneous. This woman is exhibiting the signs of preeclampsia with the hypertension, edema, headache, blurred vision, and history of diabetes. The condition is not eclampsia until accompanied by seizures. Abruptio, Previa, or supine hypotension would likely result in a low blood pressure rather than high.

Question 178: If you are preparing to perform synchronized cardioversion with this patient, what is the correct setting to start with?

c. 120J

Rationale: The recommended setting to cardiovert a patient in A-fib is 120J. Studies have shown atrial fibrillation may convert with lower Joule settings.

Question 179: You have just drawn blood from a woman who protested the whole time telling you to stop. You have just?

d. Committed battery

Rationale: You have just committed battery. You were requested to stop doing a procedure which involved touching the patient but you did not stop.

Question 180: You are called to the scene of a structure fire. Upon arrival you notice several people staggering down the block away from the fire with soot marks around their mouths. You should?

b. Call for additional ambulances and continue to assess the scene

Rationale: Getting additional help on the way to treat multiple patients is the best choice. You can treat the patients when you have determined that the scene is safe and that they are the most in need of treatment.

Question 181: You arrive on scene to find a situation that is too hazardous to enter. What should the EMT do to help ensure that the scene is not entered by unauthorized personnel?

a. Create a safety perimeter to help keep people away from the scene

Rationale: Creating a perimeter until the proper emergency teams can secure the area is the best choice. You do not want to expose yourself or crew to the hazards of the scene, so you should move to a safer area.

Question 182: Place the following steps in order for accessing a non tunneled, tunneled, and peripherally inserted CVAD:
1. Explain the procedure to the patient, clamp the catheter, and wipe the site with povidone-iodine and let dry.
2. Replace the clamp, remove syringe, connect the IV tubing to the catheter, and ensure no air is present in tubing.
3. Connect the syringe, unclamp the catheter, and draw 5 mL of blood.
4. Prepare equipment, draw 3-5mL normal saline, and put on gloves.
5. Replace the clamp, attach the syringe of normal saline to the catheter, remove the clamp and flush.
6. Remove clamp, begin infusion, tape the connection site, and administer fluid and drugs.

c. 4,1,3,5,2,6

Rationale: The order for accessing a non tunneled, tunneled, and peripherally inserted CVAD is as follows: (4) Prepare equipment, draw 3-5mL normal saline, and put on gloves. (1) Explain the procedure to the patient, clamp the catheter, wipe the site with povidone-iodine and let dry. (3) Connect the syringe, unclamp the catheter, and draw 5 mL of blood. (5) Replace the clamp, attach the syringe of normal saline to the catheter, remove the clamp, and flush. (2) Replace the clamp, remove syringe, connect the IV tubing to the catheter, and ensure no air is present in tubing. (6) Remove clamp, begin infusion, tape the connection site, and administer fluid and drugs.

Question 183: Which of the following steps are not helpful in preventing complications of vascular access devices?

c. Ensuring the patient is in semi fowler's position

Rationale: Ensuring the correct medication or nutrition is important to ensure compatibility with device. Placing a blood pressure cuff on the device can damage the device or cause complications with surrounding vasculature. Examining the device to ensure it's in proper working order before using it, is also important. Ensuring the patient is in semi fowler's position does not help prevent complications of a vascular access device.

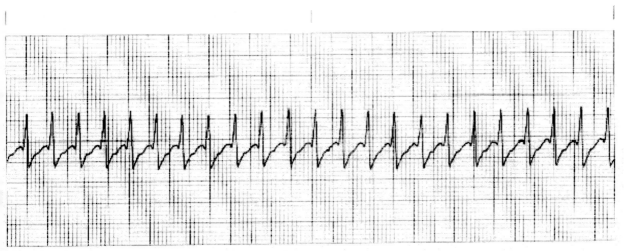

Question 184: What is your interpretation of the EKG strip above?

c. Supraventricular Tachycardia (SVT)

Rationale: Regular rhythm at 230 bpm, no visible P waves.

Question 185: Which of the following is not a complication of a central venous catheter placed in a child?

c. Slow infusion

Rationale: A dislodged or broken catheter, obstruction, and infection are all possible complications of a central venous access device placed in a child.

Question 186: You arrive on scene with your partner Steve to a Mexican restaurant where someone called in to report a choking. You enter to find a mid 30's female laying supine on the floor. She is cyanotic and unconscious. Her family says she had just taken a bite of Chimichanga when she began choking and eventually fell to the floor. What are you going to do?

b. Head tilt chin lift, verify apnea, two slow breaths, compressions, magill forceps, and laryngoscope

Rationale: Open her airway and check to see if she is breathing. If not, give two slow breaths. If you are unable to get air into the lungs in this situation, it is likely an upper airway obstruction and you should begin CPR. Each time the airway is opened to perform rescue breathing you should visually inspect the mouth for the object and remove it if seen. Proper equipment for removal would include advanced airway techniques and tools.

Question 187: The umbilical cord is wrapped tightly around the baby's neck and you have tried unsuccessfully to slip the cord over the head. What should your next course of action be?

b. Clamp the cord in two places and cut it in the middle

Rationale: Getting the baby's airway patent is the most important thing so cutting the cord appropriately would be the best decision at this point.

Question 188: When interpreting a 12-lead how do you correctly diagnose left ventricular hypertrophy?

b. Add v1's S wave in mm and the R wave in v5, if the total is greater than or equal to 35 mm the patient has left ventricular hypertrophy.

Rationale: The answer is B. Left ventricular hypertrophy means the left ventricle has dilated and thickened beyond normal level. This can be an indication your patient suffers from hypertension. Answer A is the criteria for determining right ventricular hypertrophy. The other 2 answers have no significance.

Question 189: Correctly interpret this rhythm.

a. Sinus rhythm, poor R progression, Right Bundle Branch Block with Right Axis Deviation

Rationale: The best interpretation is A. The rhythm is sinus, R progression is found in leads v1-v6, there should be a constant progression from negative R waves to positive R waves or positive to negative. In v1 there is a wide QRS (over .12) and the R wave is upright. You can also see the classic "rabbit ears". With right axis deviation you will have negative QRS in lead I and positive QRS in aVF. Answer B- If the patient had a left bundle branch block v1 would have a negative wide QRS (.12 or over) and left axis deviation is defined as an upright QRS in lead I and negative QRS in aVF. Answer C- global ST depression you would see every lead with .5mm depression.

Question 190: You and your EMT partner are dispatched to a residence of a 42-year-old male with a chief complaint of chest discomfort. When you arrive on scene you see a thin male who appears to be in relatively good shape sitting comfortably in his chair holding his chest. He tells you he is training for a marathon and just got back from running 13 miles about 30 minutes ago. While doing his cool down stretches he suddenly felt chest discomfort in the center of his chest that started radiating down his left arm. He rates the discomfort a 3 out of 10 and states he has never felt this type of discomfort before. He describes it as a dull feeling. He goes on to tell you he has been in the Olympics twice for long-distance running and tells you he is now training for the next Olympics. He states his normal heart rate is in the low 50s and has no other symptoms other than the chest discomfort. Your partner takes a baseline set of vitals and tells you his blood pressure is 110/70 and the patient is breathing 16 bpm and oxygen saturation is 98% on room air. You attach a 12-lead and hit analyze, the monitor prints this strip. What is the correct interpretation of the 12-lead?

a. Inferior MI

Rationale: The 12-lead shows a clear Inferior Myocardial Infarction. You can see ST elevation in all inferior leads II, III, and aVF of over .5mm. You can also see reciprocal changes in lateral leads I, aVL, v5, v6. The QRS in v1 is not greater then .12 so there is no indication of a left bundle branch block. With the information you have from the patient and the 12-lead findings you need to proceed as though the patient is having an active myocardial infarction. If the patient was having a Lateral MI you would see ST elevation .5mm or over in leads 1, aVL, v5, v6. An anterior MI there would be ST elevation .5mm or greater in leads v3 and v4.

Question 191: How many compressions per minute would you give an adult patient who has no pulse?

b. 100-120 compressions per minute

Rationale: 2010 AHA guidelines now require at least 100 compressions per minute, however you can do more. The best option is 100-120 compressions per minute.

Question 192: Place the following steps in order for inserting a nasogastric tube: (1) Confirm placement by auscultating the epigastrum. (2) Correctly measure from nose to ear and ear to xiphoid process. (3) Place the tube into the largest nostril and adjust to the appropriate length. (4) After attaching suction, lubricate the distal end for insertion. (5) Insert the tube down the midline into the oropharynx. (6) Inject 80-100 mL of air into the NG tube. (7) Have the patient tilt their head forward and swallow as the tube is being inserted.

a. 2,7,5,1

Rationale: The proper steps for insertion of a nasogastric tube are to correctly measure from the nose to ear and ear to xiphoid process, have the patient tilt their head forward and swallow as the tube is being inserted, insert the tube down the midline into the oropharynx, and confirm placement by auscultating the epigastrum.

Question 193: Where is a central venous catheter placed on a child?

b. Large central vein such as the subclavian

Rationale: A central venous catheter is placed on a child in a large central vein such as the subclavian. The AC doesn't give access to the central circulation, the femoral vein in the leg is preferred over the saphenous vein, and venous catheters aren't placed in arteries.

Question 194: Which of the following is a shockable rhythm?

a. VT

Rationale: Ventricular tachycardia is the only one listed that is shockable.

Question 195: You arrive on scene to find a 5-year-old child whose central venous catheter has broken, resulting in leaking fluid. What should be done for this patient?

c. Use a sterile technique to clamp off the broken line

Rationale: Using a sterile technique is important because the line accesses the central circulation. The appropriate treatment is to clamp the line stopping the leak and transport for insertion of a new line or repair of the existing line.

Question 196: A tanker truck carrying unknown chemicals has overturned on the interstate and a bright fluid is reported leaking from the truck's trailer. Several injuries are reported and many bystanders are reportedly vomiting. IC has given you the responsibility of setting up a helicopter landing zone. Which of the following potential areas would be the most appropriate for this zone?

a. A slight slope approximately 80 feet X 80 feet that is uphill and upwind of the hazardous incident

Rationale: You would want to choose a location that is uphill and upwind of the scene. You would also not want to land the helicopter in a place that was evacuated because of vomiting.

Question 197: Which of the following is not used for airway maintenance and ventilation?

d. DAP

Rationale: DAP is made up. The others are oropharyngeal, nasopharyngeal, and bag valve mask. All are used for the question.

Question 198: Hypothermia is diagnosed when the body's organs are below what temperature?

c. 95 degrees

Rationale: When the body's organs are below 95 degrees, it is considered hypothermia.

Question 199: You arrive on scene to find a 35 year-old-male complaining of a burning pain in the left upper quadrant, vomiting blood, and melena. Which of the following is the likely cause of these symptoms?

d. Peptic Ulcer Disease

Rationale: Peptic Ulcer disease is when ulcers are formed in the lining of the stomach or duodenum where acid and pepsin are present. The pain is typically described as burning in the left upper quadrant. The patient may also complain of vomiting blood and black tarry stools. Appendicitis is when an obstruction of the passageway between the appendix and cecum or inflammation occurs. The pain is typically in the lower right quadrant and is accompanied by cramping, nausea, vomiting, and chills. Diverticulitis occurs when fecal matter obstructs one or more diverticula. The pain is typically found in the lower left quadrant and accompanied by irregular bowel habits and fever. Ulcerative Colitis is an inflammatory condition of the large intestine. Common symptoms include fatigue, weight loss, bleeding of the rectum, and in some cases severe abdominal cramping.

Question 200: An explosion has occurred at a nearby petroleum refinery. Incident Command has appointed you as the triage officer. What color triage tag would each of the following patients receive? Patient 1 is a 9 year old female with a broken arm. She is breathing at 8 breaths a minute. Patient 2 is an elderly male with a compound fracture of the left femur. He is in decompensated shock from loss of blood and has no pulse. Patient 3 is an elderly man who has a laceration on his forehead and a GCS of 8. Patient 4 is a 5 year old male breathing at 18 breaths a minute with a head contusion.

b. 1Red, 2Black, 3Red, 4Green

Rationale: The first patient is priority 1 or red tagged because of the bradypnea. Patient 2 is a black tag because he has no pulse and is likely in an unrecoverable state. Patient 3 is red tagged because of the diminished LOC. Patient 4 is a green tag because he only has a bump on the head.

Question 201: Where is a non-tunneled CVAD inserted?

d. Through the skin into the subclavian vein

Rationale: A non-tunneled CVAD or Central Venous Access Device is inserted through the skin into the internal jugular, subclavian, cephalic, brachial, femoral, or basilic veins. The goal is placing the tip of the device into the superior or inferior vena cava, accessing the central circulation. Although cannulation of the antecubital vein accesses venous circulation, it's not central circulation. The other choices are inappropriate.

Question 202: Poor R wave progression on a 12-lead can be caused by all of the following except?

a. Myocardial Ischemia

Rationale: In Normal R wave progression, the R wave starts out negative in V1 and continuously progresses to a positive R wave in V6. There is usually a transition from negative to positive QRS in leads V3 or V4. Myocardial Ischemia is not a reason for poor R wave progression.

Question 203: You and your partner Pepe arrive on scene to find a man in his early twenties with a large gash on his forearm that is spurting blood. You immediately apply pressure with your gloved hand as Pepe hands you a trauma dressing. The patient is pale with a weak rapid pulse and respirations of 30 breaths per minute. As you are finishing your initial assessment and bandaging the wound the PT tells you to "get away" from him. Your best course of action would be to do what?

b. Explain to the patient that you are almost finished bandaging his wound and you will leave him alone then

Rationale: If you continue to treat a patient who is refusing treatment you can be charged with assault and or battery. Do your best to finish up the treatment, but if the patient continues to refuse, you must comply.

Question 204: You and your partner Toby arrive at a motel in response to a 911 call for an unconscious female. You find the woman pulseless and while Toby hooks up the AED, you begin delivering compressions. How many compressions per minute would you give this woman?

b. 100-109 compressions per minute

Rationale: 100-109 compressions per minute would satisfy AHA CPR Guidelines which state that AT LEAST 100 compressions per minute should be delivered.

Question 205: History and assessment findings for hypoglycemia may include of all of the following except:

a. polyuria

Rationale: History and assessment findings for hypoglycemia may include: Onset - rapid changes in mental status; bizarre behavior, tremors, shaking; sweating, hunger; rapid full pulse, rapid shallow respirations; seizures, coma late; and medical alert identification.

Question 206: You have requested helicopter transportation of a critical burn patient. The remote nature of the accident will force the helicopter to land on an incline. From which direction should you approach the helicopter?

d. The downhill side

Rationale: Approaching from the downhill side of the helicopter is the safest route in this situation.

Question 207: You arrive on scene to a 62 year old male with chief complaint of hematemesis. The patient is sitting on the couch with a large bucket in front of him violently vomiting bright red blood. You take the appropriate BSI precautions and ask the patient when this began. He explains he has been an alcoholic for 30 years and this happens from time to time. What is this patient most likely suffering from, and how would you treat him?

d. Esophageal Varices- Ensure the patient continues to have an airway, start an IV, begin a fluid resuscitation, transport.

Rationale: This patient is most likely suffering from Esophageal varices. The key is that he has been an alcoholic for 30 years and is vomiting bright red blood. Treatment includes managing airway and fluid administration. Inserting a nasogastric tube in someone with Esophageal varices is controversial and usually not recommended. Pancreatitis can cause vomiting and severe pain but not usually bright red blood. Crohn's disease is a chronic inflammatory disease of the bowels. Gastroenteritis is an infection of the stomach and intestines, which can cause diarrhea and vomiting but not usually bright red blood with melena.

Question 208: You are dispatched to an accident involving two semi trucks and several cars that have collided under an overpass. The reporting party says that there are several people in the road and nobody is helping them. Your unit is the first to arrive on scene. After performing a thorough scene size-up, what should you do?

c. Assume command of the scene

Rationale: The first functional role that must be filled is that of the Incident Commander. You must assume that role, and more than likely will also immediately fill the role of Triage Officer as well. However, you must establish command so that the incident can be managed properly. A scene that has no IC will quickly become chaotic and dangerous.

Question 209: The 2010 ACLS guidelines recommend the temperature of the fluid used when inducing hypothermia during post-cardiac arrest care to be?

b. 4 Degrees Celsius

Rationale: ACLS guidelines state during post-cardiac arrest care to use fluid at a temperature of 4 Degrees Celsius when inducing hypothermia.

Question 210: You arrive on scene to find a 22 year old male complaining of intense lower right quadrant abdominal cramping. Upon further examination you discover that prior to the severe cramping he had slight cramping, nausea, vomiting, a fever. Which of the following condtions is most likely the cause?

c. Appendicitis

Rationale: Appendicitis occurs in 7-10% of the population in the United States and typically occurs between the ages of 8-25. The first signs may be hard to differentiate, as they are present with several conditions. These symptoms include cramping or pain in the abdomen, nausea, vomiting, chills, or a low grade fever. Later on the pain becomes more severe and is typically present in the lower right quadrant. Crohn's Disease is an inflammatory, chronic bowel disease, which can result in blockage of the intestine due to swelling of the intestinal wall. The symptoms include excessive diarrhea, severe abdominal pain, weight loss, and weakness. Hemorrhoids are veins that have become swollen or distended in or around the skin of the anus. A sign of a hemmorhoid is bleeding from the anus after defecation. Hepatitis is the result of the liver being inflamed. Acute Hepatitis is characterized by the sudden onset of symptoms such as malaise, weakness, nausea or vomiting, and pain in the upper right quadrant.

Question 211: When transmitting a number with two or more digits you should say the whole number first, followed by:

b. Saying each number individually

Rationale: Proper radio transmission protocols would call for saying each number individually as in, "seventy five - seven five."

Question 212: A woman's obstetrical history can be displayed using P and G. How would you display a woman's history who has had 3 pregnancies and 2 live births?

d. G3P2

Rationale: G3P2 would denote Gravida or number of pregnancies and Para or number of live births.

Question 213: Medical control is responsible for all of the following EXCEPT:

c. Getting the patient to the hospital safely and quickly

Rationale: Medical control is rarely, if ever, on scene. It is your responsibility to ensure safe and rapid transport of the patient.

Question 214: What disease is caused from abnormally high levels of corticosteroid hormones produced by the adrenal glands? It can cause increased facial hair, weight gain, muscle atrophy, and a moon face appeerence.

d. Cushing Syndrome

Rationale: Cushing syndrome is a disease caused by high levels of corticosteroid produced by the adrenal glands. It can be caused by a tumor on the adrenal glands or pituitary glands or administration of corticosteroid drugs. Addison disease is the opposite of Cushings and is deficiency of corticosteroids in the adrenal glands. Myxedema is commonly an inflammation of the thyroid or from treatment for hypothyroidism, it is a deficiency in thyroid hormone. Grave disease is an autoimmune disorder that leads to overactivity of the thyroid gland. Cushing's syndrome is not to be mistaken for Cushing's triad.

Question 215: You arrive on scene to find a 26-year-old male with a red, swollen eye who is complaining of pain and a scratching feeling. After interviewing him, he believes a piece of metal flew into his eye while he was grinding metal. What is the best treatment for the patient?

c. Bandage the eye and transport

Rationale: When an object is embedded in the eye the best treatment is bandaging the eye and transport. Flushing the eye is appropriate if a liquid or powder substance has splashed into the eye.

Question 216: When is an infant considered premature?

d. All of the above

Rationale: Any baby born before the 37th week is considered premature, all of the answers are correct.

Question 217: It's 4:30 p.m., you and your partner Jim are called to a motor vehicle accident on a busy side street. You arrive on scene and can see at least 6 patients from 4 cars. The cars are a twisted mess and are covering one whole lane of traffic with multiple fluids pooling around the cars. You can hear people crying and traffic is already starting to move around and by the wreck. You should...?

b. Assure the fire department is en route, establish a safety zone, and assist in keeping traffic at a safe distance

Rationale: Scene safety before all else in this case. The best thing you can do for everybody is help to keep the accident from getting even larger. Assist with traffic and crowd control until the proper authorities get there. Then you can administer medical attention in a safe environment.

Question 218: You arrive on scene to find a woman in her 20's who phoned in her own diabetic emergency. She is now unconscious and breathing at 20 a minute with a pulse of 110. She told the dispatcher on the phone that she had hypoglycemia and had not eaten that day. Your best course of treatment would include?

d. Obtain a blood sugar, O2 via NRB at 15 lpm, and Initiate an IV of D5W

Rationale: Administering D5 via IV would be the best choice from the options given.

Question 219: What is the area of hazardous contamination known as?

c. Hot zone

Rationale: An area of contamination is referred to as the hot zone.

Question 220: You arrive on scene to find a 57 year old man who is sitting on a couch appearing to stare at the wall. His breathing is labored and you can hear wet breath sounds that are producing a pink foam dripping from his mouth. You get no response when you try to get his name. Your requests for him to move his arm go without response. His pulse is 105 and his BP is 92/40. You do not see any edema, swelling, or JVD. This patient likely has _____.

a. Left sided CHF

Rationale: Left sided Congestive Heart Failure typically produces crackles or wet lung sounds and is accompanied by pink foamy sputum. With right sided CHF you would expect to see edema, swelling, or distended jugular veins because of the back up of fluids into the vasculature.

Question 221: Pancuronium is classified as what type of medication?

d. Non-depolarizing neuromuscular blocker

Rationale: Pancuronium competes with acetycholine receptor sites which results in the paralysis of muscle fibers. Pancuronium does not cause an initial depolarization wave, thus it is non-depolarizing.

Question 222: A 26 year old woman has called the ambulance because she has begun delivery of her baby. Dispatch says the mother stated the baby's foot was sticking out of the vaginal opening. You should be prepared to?

b. Place patient into a knee to chest position and rapid transport

Rationale: Allow gravity to assist you in keeping the child in the canal until definitive care.

Question 223: You are ventilating an intubated patient en route to the hospital. You have attached capnography and after a few minutes notice this waveform. What is the first thing you should do?

d. Check placement of ET tube

Rationale: The most common reason for a waveform to suddenly drop and go flat is due to an ET tube being displaced. Immediately check placement of the ET tube to confirm it wasn't dislodged from the trachea.

Question 224: You arrive on scene to find a 25 year old female complaining of fatigue, rectal bleeding, and nausea. After evaluating her you discover she has also had bloody diarrhea and a fever. Which of the following conditions would cause these symptoms?

a. Ulcerative Colitis

Rationale: Ulcerative Colitis is an inflammatory condition of the large intestine. The disease occurs most commonly between the ages of 15-30 and occurs equally in men and women. Common symptoms include fatigue, weight loss, and bleeding of the rectum. More severe symptoms include bloody diarrhea, nausea, and severe cramping. Mallory-Weiss Syndrome occurs when the inner lining of the esophagus tears where it connects to the stomach. Symptoms include vomiting blood or passing black sticky stools after a period of coughing, retching, or vomiting. Acute Gastroenteritis is when the stomach or intestines become inflamed after a sudden onset of vomiting or diarrhea. Acute Gastroenteritis is typically caused by an infection (bacterial or viral). Pancreatitis is when the pancreas becomes inflamed. Symptoms include severe abdominal pain, nausea, vomiting, and abdominal distension.

Question 225: Which solution has the same osmotic pressure as the fluids in the human body?

a. Isotonic

Rationale: An isotonic solution has the same osmotic pressure. Hyper has more and hypo has less.

Question 226: When would a nasogastric tube be used over an orogastric tube?

c. In a conscious patient with severe nausea

Rationale: An NG tube is preferred over an OG tube when a patient is conscious. An NG tube can mistakenly be placed intracranially with facial trauma. An airway occlusion shouldn't hinder NG tube placement as long as the occlusion isn't large enough to block the esophagus too.

Question 227: According to AHA CPR and AED guidelines, a patient with a VF rhythm should be shocked how many times before CPR is resumed?

a. 1

Rationale: AHA recommendations are for 1 shock followed by CPR. Studies found that 85% of patients with VF were converted on the first shock.

Question 228: Assessment findings and symptoms for a patient that has taken a hallucinogen include all of the following except:

b. Lacrimation

Rationale: Assessment findings and symptoms for a patient that has taken hallucinogen include: hallucinations, intensified vision, intensified hearing, separation from reality, hypertensive, tachycardia, anxiousness, and paranoia.

Question 229: You arrive on scene of a one-car motor vehicle accident. A single female patient can be observed in the car having breathing difficulties. You notice power lines are down across the hood of the car but you do not see any sparks. What would be your best course of action?

b. Notify the power company and keep a safe distance until they have removed the wires

Rationale: You need to be positive the scene is safe. Remember, the absence of sparks does not mean the wires are not charged. You should never approach a vehicle that has power lines over it until you are assured by the utility company that there is no risk for electric shock.

Question 230: You arrive on scene of a 54 year old female with 8 out of 10 chest pain. She denies cardiac history and reports the pain started while cooking dinner. She describes the pain as dull and non-radiating. Your partner obtains a baseline set of vitals while you perform a 12 lead ECG. You notice 2mm ST elevation in leads II, III, and aVF. What type of infarction is this patient having?

c. Inferior Infarction

Rationale: ST elevation in leads II, III, and aVF mean the patient is having an inferior infarction. If the patient was having a septal infarction you would see ST elevation in leads v1 and v2. ST elevation in leads v3 and v4 mean they are having an anterior infarction, and leads v5 and v6 indicate a lateral infarction.

Question 231: You arrive on scene for a possible poisoning. The patient is a 9 month old girl who was found with an open bottle of drain cleaner. She has a bump on her forehead and is noticeably irritable. During your assessment you note that the child does not make eye contact with you at all. Which of the following is the best course of action and why?

a. Initiate transport with blow by oxygen. The lack of eye contact and irritability are concerning signs in children this age.

Rationale: A child who is not making eye contact and acting irritable with a possible head or ingestion emergency should be transported immediately and given oxygen. Blow-by is an appropriate oxygen treatment for children.

Question 232: What usually happens to the ventricles of the heart when Adenosine is administered to a patient for SVT?

d. It causes ventricular asystole for a short period of time

Rationale: Adenosine blocks the AV node. After you administer it to the patient, watch the EKG and you will usually see asystole for a short period of time, up to 30 seconds. It can make you a little nervous because the patient is usually alert and oriented through this process.

Question 233: Your patient is an 8 year old girl who fell from a swing and hit her head. She has a pulse but is not breathing. Your CPR should include what?

a. Breaths at a rate of 12-20

Rationale: AHA Guidelines specify that for all children, a rescue breath rate of 12-20 is to be used.

Question 234: When using waveform capnography during post-cardiac arrest care you will ventilate the patient to achieve a PETCO2 reading of_____mm Hg?

d. 35-40

Rationale: According to 2010 ACLS guidelines when treating a post-cardiac arrest patient you want to maintain PETCO2 reading of 35-40 mm Hg, which can be seen by using waveform capnography.

Question 235: How many beats a minute would constitute bradycardia in a school-aged child?

b. Less than 70

Rationale: A school-aged child would be considered bradycardic if their heart rate was less than 70.

Question 236: You are performing CPR on a man in cardiac arrest. Which of the following choices would you administer first?

d. Vasopressin 40 units Vasopressin 40 units

Rationale: According to 2010 guidelines the first line drugs for a patient in cardiac arrest are Epinephrine (1:10,000) 1mg or Vasopressin 40 units. Vasopressin can replace Epinephrine in the first or second dose, and can only be given once. Atropine is no longer recommended in cardiac arrest patients.

Question 237: You connect a 4-lead EKG to a patient and observe sinus bradycardia. You decide to administer Atropine per protocol. What is the maximum dose of Atropine you can administer to a patient?

a. 3mg

Rationale: According to 2010 ACLS guidelines, the dosage for Atropine is .5mg every 3-5 minutes, for a maximum dosage of 3mg. Every drug in ACLS and PALS can be used in the NREMT exams. Know your stuff!!!

Question 238: Your partner is ventilating a patient with a BVM after return of spontaneous circulation. You have this waveform showing on your monitor. What are your instructions to your partner regarding the ventilation rate.

c. Continue same ventilation rate

Rationale: Advise your partner to continue the same ventilation rate. A normal wave form will begin at the base line, raise steeply, plateau with a gradual upslope, and will quickly return to the baseline. The normal end tidal CO2 reading is between 35-40 mm Hg. Note: Analyze capnography wave form like an EKG interpretation, with a systematic approach. 1. Is there CO2 present, this can be seen by the presence of a wave form. 2. Does the waveform rise steeply, plateau with a gradual upslope, and then quickly return to baseline. 3. Look at the respiratory base line, does the end tidal CO2 wave form return to zero during inhalation? If not, then you know there is a complication.

Question 239: You have been called to a home where a 1-year-old girl is in respiratory distress, possible apnea. The caregiver called 911 after finding the girl on the floor in front of the T.V. She does not know if the child is breathing or not. Which of the following choices below contains the most accurate facts related to this call?

a. Children have a large tongue that takes up more of the oropharynx and can cause an airway obstruction. Proper administration of CPR should include about an inch of padding under the child's shoulders.

Rationale: Children have a larger tongue in proportion to their oropharnyx than adults. This makes it easy for a childs tongue to occlude their airway and cause an obstruction. Proper positioning of the airway will help reduce this. One way to position the child for proper airway alignment, if performing assisted or artificial ventilations during CPR, is to place padding under the child's shoulders to help put the airway in a neutral position.

Question 240: You arrive on scene to an MVA involving 1 car with 3 passengers. Which of the following signs would most increase your suspicion that the driver may have significant internal injuries?

a. The passenger in the front is dead.

Rationale: While all of the answer choices contain signs that may lead you to believe that the MOI was significant, the presence of the dead passenger is the most telling sign that the mechanism was significant enough to cause internal injuries to the driver.

Question 241: According to the American Heart Association what is the first alternative if intravenous access fails?

c. Intraosseous Route

Rationale: According to the AHA if intravenous access is not feasible or possible then intraosseous (IO) route should be attempted next. The IO route is an injection into the bone marrow cavity. This in general is a quick and safe alternative.

Question 242: What is the correct interpretation and conduction rate of this rhythm strip?

b. A-flutter - 3:1 conduction

Rationale: The correct rhythm is A-flutter, which is a regular rate with saw tooth or picket fence waves. The most common type of A-flutter is 2:1 conduction, however, as in this picture it can be 3:1, and can also be 4:1 or more.

Question 243: A man has burns all over his head as well as over his entire genitalia, but nowhere else on his body. What percentage of the man's body is burned according to the rule of nines?

b. 10 Percent

Rationale: The head is 9% plus 1% for genitalia.

Question 244: What is the best description of how Adenosine affects the heart?

a. Blocks electrical activity in the AV node

Rationale: Answer 'A' best describes the affect Adenosine has on the heart. Adenosine blocks electrical activity in the AV node causing ventricular asystole for a few seconds. Adenosine is not a Calcium Channel Blocker. B. is a description of Diltiazem, C. is a description of Atropine, and D. is a description of Epinephrine. Notice all of these drugs are ACLS drugs. It would be helpful to know these in preperation for your testing.

Question 245: You arrive on scene to find a female patient actively having contractions every 10-12 minutes apart. A visual inspection of the patient reveals no visible crowning. Which stage of labor would you consider this patient to be in?

a. 1st stage of labor.

Rationale: The first stage of labor is dilation of the cervix. This can have contractions at varying intervals, and can also have some blood spotting or the breaking of the 'waters'. It ends when the cervix is fully dilated. The second stage of labor begins at that point and continues until the baby has been fully delivered. The third stage is the delivery of the umbilicus and placenta. The fourth stage is usually referred to as the period of time after delivery of the placenta and is not referenced in all textbooks. In the pre-hospital setting it is difficult to know if your patient is still in the first or second stage of labor since we don't check for cervical dilation. One good way to know is to understand that the urge to push comes after the cervix is dilated, so this is a great indicator that the patient has moved beyond stage 1 and is now in stage 2.

Question 246: What is the generic name for Versed?

b. Midazolam

Rationale: Midazolam is the generic name for Versed. Lorazepam is the generic name for Ativan. Diazepam is the generic name for Valium, and Alprazolam is the generic name for Xanax. You will notice that all of the generic names end with "am," this is a common theme with benzodiazepines. Versed, Ativan, and Valium are common benzo's used in EMS. Versed is used for sedation and impairs memory. It is commonly used to control seizures, pain management, and pre-sedation cardioversion and intubation. Xanax is a common presecription drug for anxiety, and you may see the generic name on medication lists for patients.

Question 247: A patient with pulmonary edema that presents with shortness of breath and crackles would best benefit from which of the following?

a. Continuous positive airway pressure

Rationale: Pulmonary edema or a buildup of fluid in the air sacks of the lungs leads to shortness of breath. CPAP is the most beneficial as it reduces the work of breathing while splinting airways open to facilitate gas exchange. Intubation is your last resort. A Duoneb treatment is for airway constriction not edema, and PEEP allows the alveoli to remain open during exhalation.

Question 248: You are dispatched to the scene of an unconscious woman. Upon arrival you are confronted by a 35 year old man who is very upset and appears to have the mental capacity of a 10 year old. He takes you by the hand and leads you into the bedroom where his mother, a woman in her 70s is sitting in a chair unresponsive. The man wants to know if his mother is ok and why she won't speak. You should?

a. Tell the man you are going to take care of his mother and that he may ride in the ambulance with her to the hospital

Rationale: Situations like these are not as uncommon as you might think. The best choice of answer would be to give the man assurance without lying and allow him to accompany his mother to the ER.

Question 249: Stimulation of alpha receptors will likely?

c. Constrict blood vessels

Rationale: Alpha receptor stimulation will cause the blood vessels to constrict. Blockage of the receptor would have the opposite effect

Question 250: You arrive on scene to a patient who has been having seizures for over 3 minutes. You have been ordered to start an IV and administer 2mg of Lorazepam. What drug are you going to give?

b. Ativan

Rationale: Lorazepam is the generic name for Ativan. Midazolam is the generic name for Versed. Diazepam is the generic name for Valium, and Morphine sulfate is known simply as Morphine sulfate. You will notice that all of the generic names end with "am," this is a common theme with benzodiazepines. Versed, Ativan, and Valium are common benzo's used in EMS. Ativan is a common drug used for status epilepticus or recurrent seizures and anxiety. It acts by depressing the CNS, it also has anti-convulsant and sedation properties.

CPSIA information can be obtained at www.ICGtesting.com
Printed in the USA
LVOW09s1620131014

408533LV00016B/724/P